FAMOUS BIDDING DECISIONS

For this exciting book Terence Reese and David Bird have selected sixty celebrated bidding decisions. The authors have ingeniously presented them so that after seeing how the key point in the auction was reached you can take over and exercise your own skill. As would be expected, the commentary on the bidding from these two redoubtable exponents fairly crackles with vitality and by the end of the book your game will be considerably rejuvenated.

Terence Reese and David Bird were described by *The Bridge World* as 'having scored a bull's eye' with *That Elusive Extra Trick*, which dealt with card play. This challenging new title completes the double.

> 'Watch closely now, *very* closely. *Famous Bidding Decisions* is an excellent collection of deals from major events, displaying the talents (and, occasionally, the mishaps) of many of the world's best players. Most of the 60 articles highlight an instructive or unusual *card play* situation. As the authors' eye for interesting positions is outstanding, and the selection ranges widely over both time and locale, this is a worthy collection; the book receives our endorsement on this aspect alone.'
>
> *The Bridge World*

FAMOUS BIDDING DECISIONS

Test Your Skill Against the Experts

Terence Reese & David Bird

CASSELL&CO
IN ASSOCIATION WITH
PETER CRAWLEY

First published in Great Britain 1996
In association with Peter Crawley
by Victor Gollancz
Second impression 2001
published in association with Peter Crawley
by Cassell and Co
Wellington House, 125 Strand, London WC2R 0BB
a division of the Orion Publishing Group

ISBN 0-304-35775-8

Printed and Bound in Great Britain by
Mackays of Chatham, Kent.

Contents

PART III   THE COMPETITIVE AUCTION

Foreword

Each of the sixty deals described in this book contains a 'famous bidding decision'. The scene is set, the bidding decision presented, and you are invited to select from a short-list of possible calls. You may then turn the page to compare your decision with that of the original player and see how your chosen action would have fared. At the same time we assess each call, awarding marks out of a possible 5.

When the deals – many of them from world championship play – first arose, the various bidding decisions resulted in swings totalling some 700 IMPs. Several of them actually affected the result of the championship. The deals we have chosen nearly all contain a point of interest in the play, too.

At the risk of sounding like two unpopular schoolmasters, may we suggest that you take some time to estimate the alternatives on each deal, then *write down* what seems to you to be the best answer. Only then turn over and see what happened and what we recommend.

The book is divided into three sections. In the first, the bidding problems have been caused by enemy pre-emption. The second part contains problems in constructive auctions, the opponents remaining silent. The final part covers the all-out warfare of competitive bidding, in particular decisions at a high level: should you bid one more, double the opponents, or perhaps pass? Even the world's best sometimes fall off their pedestals and we believe you will often find a better answer than the original contestants!

Terence Reese
David Bird

PART I THE OPPONENTS PRE-EMPT

Many testing decisions arise when the opponents pre-empt,
denying you bidding space. Sometimes it is a guessing game but
good judgement will always play a part.

1. Dramatic Ending

Italy and Great Britain contested an exciting semi-final in the 1964
Olympiad, played in New York. On the last board North–South
were vulnerable and North held:

$$\spadesuit \; Q$$
$$\heartsuit \; 10\,7\,3\,2$$
$$\diamondsuit \; K\,J\,2$$
$$\clubsuit \; Q\,10\,9\,8\,6$$

Your right-hand opponent opens a weak two hearts, which is
followed by two passes. Your partner now springs to life with a
cue-bid of three hearts:

SOUTH	WEST	NORTH	EAST
	2♡	Pass	Pass
3♡	Pass	?	

How should you react? If you think your heart holding will
form a sufficient stop, combined with whatever partner may hold
in the suit, you can try 3NT. Instead you could simply show your
best suit at the minimum level – four clubs. If you think it
appropriate to show that you have a few useful cards, you could
jump to five clubs or perhaps cue-bid four hearts.

It's hard to think of anything else, so you may award marks out
of 5 to these options:

(1) 3NT   (2) 4♣   (3) 4♡   (4) 5♣

North–South game
Dealer West

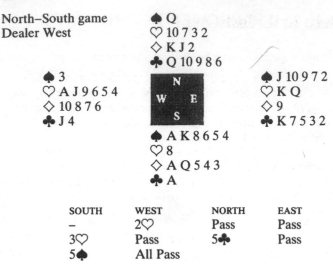

♠ Q
♡ 10 7 3 2
◇ K J 2
♣ Q 10 9 8 6

♠ 3
♡ A J 9 6 5 4
◇ 10 8 7 6
♣ J 4

♠ J 10 9 7 2
♡ K Q
◇ 9
♣ K 7 5 3 2

♠ A K 8 6 5 4
♡ 8
◇ A Q 5 4 3
♣ A

SOUTH	WEST	NORTH	EAST
–	2♡	Pass	Pass
3♡	Pass	5♣	Pass
5♠	All Pass		

Leslie Dodds, North, chose to show some values with a leap to five clubs. Harrison Gray now had to play in five spades and, with the spades breaking badly, could not avoid the loss of two spades and a heart – one down. At the other table the Italians reached the fine contract of six diamonds, but after a heart lead the bad breaks put this three down. Had Dodds and Gray stopped in four spades the British team would have qualified for the final, in which Italy beat the USA by a big margin.

Some pundits at the time were inclined to blame Gray, saying that he might have bid three spades or four spades at his first turn. That makes no sense at all; Gray had a fine three-loser hand, with every chance of a slam. As we see it, the fault lies with North. South would double on any three-suited hand, so he was marked with a two-suiter (or conceivably a freak one-suiter). There was no need at all for North to jump in response. If a fit came to light after a four-club response he could show signs of life then, if need be. We mark it:

3NT–0,   4♣–5,   4♡–2,   5♣–1

Nowadays most players would double on the South cards, rather than start with a cue-bid. This will yield a big penalty when partner has something useful in hearts over declarer. When partner instead makes some response or other, there will be more room to investigate than there would be after the cue-bid.

2. Seen in a Flash

At one time there was a fashion for Par Contests. Testing hands were prepared and players could score points for both bidding and play (always in the 'directed' contract). Nowadays no-one seems to have the energy to prepare a good set; admittedly, it was always a difficult and laborious task.

Two Australians, M. J. Sullivan and R. E. Williams, composed the deals for two world-wide Par Olympiads. There were many good hands in these, but a slight failing was that the bidding and play did not always 'mix' well. You will see an example of this on a deal where North, vulnerable against not, held:

♠ A 5 4 3 2
♡ J 3 2
◇ 4 3
♣ A 4 2

The bidding begins:

SOUTH	WEST	NORTH	EAST
–	5♣	Pass	Pass
Dble	Pass	?	

Partner's double shows a strong hand in general and there is no reason to expect he will hold anything much in clubs. You could leave in the double if you don't expect to score much, playing the hand your way. You could take out into five spades or you could head for a slam.

If you are thinking of a slam, six clubs would perhaps be a more prepared effort than a direct jump to six spades. You may award the usual points out of 5 for these calls:

(1) Pass   (2) 5♠   (3) 6♣   (4) 6♠

North–South game
Dealer West

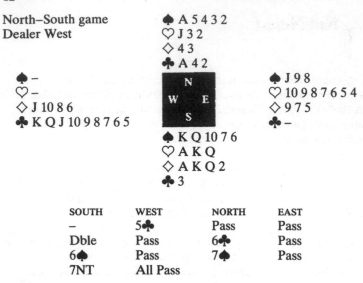

♠ A 5 4 3 2
♡ J 3 2
◇ 4 3
♣ A 4 2

♠ –
♡ –
◇ J 10 8 6
♣ K Q J 10 9 8 7 6 5

♠ J 9 8
♡ 10 9 8 7 6 5 4
◇ 9 7 5
♣ –

♠ K Q 10 7 6
♡ A K Q
◇ A K Q 2
♣ 3

SOUTH	WEST	NORTH	EAST
–	5♣	Pass	Pass
Dble	Pass	6♣	Pass
6♠	Pass	7♠	Pass
7NT	All Pass		

South's double does not promise such a giant as he actually held. Nevertheless, with two precious aces, North can visualise a slam. Six spades is more or less justified on the values but may not be the right suit. Best is six clubs, though you may still have an awkward decision on the next round. We make it:

Pass–0,   5♠–1,   6♠–3,   6♣–5

The 'recommended bidding' in the Par Contest had North raising to seven spades when his partner unexpectedly bid six spades over six clubs. Somewhat of a view to take! Fearing a possible club ruff in that contract, South converts to 7NT. (Well, the problem setters had to get them there somehow . . .)

West leads ♣K, won by the ace, and East discards a heart. Declarer must realise that his only chance for thirteen tricks lies in a diamond–club squeeze against West. In other words, West must hold 0–0–4–9 shape. So that he can be in dummy when the squeeze is about to start, South must finesse ♠10 at trick two, cash the king–queen of spades, three top hearts, and ♠7. Then a spade to the ace twists West's arm. Terence Reese's partner, Claude Rodrigue (warned, he said, by the uncompromising ♠ A 5 4 3 2 in dummy), saw this in the proverbial flash.

3.   Not Noted

With one round to play in the 1972 World Mixed Teams championship, two US teams were well ahead of the field. Wolff led Roth by 4 VPs. The Roth team had to face Forquet's Italian squad in its last match. On one board, at Love All, Forquet held these cards as South:

♠ 5
♡ A K J 10 2
♢ A 5
♣ A J 4 3 2

Barbara Rappaport opened a weak two spades on his left and after two passes he doubled. His partner, Anna Valenti, responded three diamonds, so these were the early exchanges:

SOUTH	WEST	NORTH	EAST
Forquet	Rappaport	Valenti	Roth
–	2♠	Pass	Pass
Dble	Pass	3♢	Pass
?			

What would your next move be? You could pass or bid three hearts. If you regard your hand more highly you might jump to four hearts, or perhaps cue-bid three spades. This is the list:

(1) Pass   (2) 3♡   (3) 3♠   (4) 4♡

Love all
Dealer West

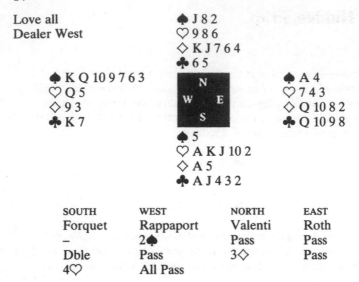

♠ J 8 2
♡ 9 8 6
◇ K J 7 6 4
♣ 6 5

♠ K Q 10 9 7 6 3
♡ Q 5
◇ 9 3
♣ K 7

♠ A 4
♡ 7 4 3
◇ Q 10 8 2
♣ Q 10 9 8

♠ 5
♡ A K J 10 2
◇ A 5
♣ A J 4 3 2

SOUTH	WEST	NORTH	EAST
Forquet	Rappaport	Valenti	Roth
–	2♠	Pass	Pass
Dble	Pass	3◇	Pass
4♡	All Pass		

Forquet, visualising a game opposite as little as ♣ Q 10, jumped to 4♡. This was a slight overbid and 3♡ would have been a slight underbid. In deference to the Italian maestro we mark it:

Pass–0,   3♡–4,   3♠–0,   4♡–5

Forquet ruffed the second spade and played ace and another club, to West's king. West continued with ♠Q, East throwing a diamond and South ruffing again. Forquet cashed the ace and king of diamonds, ruffed a diamond with the ace and led a third round of clubs. Had West ruffed with the queen, this would have ended the defence. She discarded, though, and Forquet ruffed in the dummy. A trump finesse lost, West returned a trump, and that was one down.

It was not noted at the time, but suppose Forquet had cashed the diamonds in a different order – the king, then the ace. If West discards on the third club declarer will ruff low, ruff a diamond with the ace, and lead another club. If West declines to ruff again, declarer will ruff in the dummy, ruff a diamond with the heart king, and continue to crossruff. The defenders take only the queen of trumps.

4. Hidden Trap

Star-studded teams that include a wealthy sponsor are a way of life in the US. Indeed one or two have gone on to become world champions. On the present deal Fejervary, the sponsor of the 1975 Spingold winners, was sitting South for his team in the US trials for the Bermuda Bowl. He held:

> ♠ A K Q J 5 4
> ♡ 4 2
> ◇ A 7 3 2
> ♣ J

At Game All his right-hand opponent opened five clubs. Five spades would be rather adventurous and Fejervary contented himself with a double. Further developments were in store:

SOUTH	WEST	NORTH	EAST
–	–	–	5♣
Dble	Pass	6♡	Pass
?			

What now? If partner has as much as ♡ A K Q J x and the club ace, a grand slam will be on. His leap to six could be based on a quite different hand, though, maybe a longer heart suit without the club ace. If you reckon that the six level will be high enough, you still have to decide whether to leave six hearts or correct to six spades.

These are the options:

> (1) Pass   (2) 6♠   (3) 7♡   (4) 7♠

Game all   ♠ 2
Dealer East   ♡ A K Q 9 6 5 3
                ◇ J 6 4
                ♣ Q 10

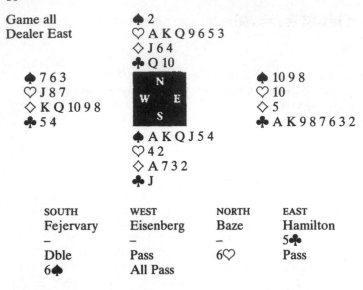

♠ 7 6 3   ♠ 10 9 8
♡ J 8 7   ♡ 10
◇ K Q 10 9 8   ◇ 5
♣ 5 4   ♣ A K 9 8 7 6 3 2

                ♠ A K Q J 5 4
                ♡ 4 2
                ◇ A 7 3 2
                ♣ J

SOUTH	WEST	NORTH	EAST
Fejervary	Eisenberg	Baze	Hamilton
–	–	–	5♣
Dble	Pass	6♡	Pass
6♠	All Pass		

Bidding a grand would be somewhat wild and since six hearts
and six spades appear equally cold, you may not consider this
much of a 'Famous Bidding Decision'. Six spades presented a trap
in the play, however.

Declarer ruffed the second club and drew trumps, finding them
3–3. That gave East eleven cards in the black suits. He followed
to ◇A too, leaving only one unknown card in his hand. If this
was a diamond, a first-round finesse of dummy's ♡9 would be
needed. Fejervary drew breath and bravely finessed dummy's ♡9,
losing to the 10. At the other table North made six hearts to land
17 IMPs.

South had promised nothing in hearts and should not have
disturbed 6♡. On a minor-suit lead six spades would be hopeless
opposite such as: ♠x ♡ K Q J x x x x x ◇ x x ♣ A x. We make
it:

$$\text{Pass–5,} \quad 6♠-2, \quad 7♡-0, \quad 7♠-1$$

Did you spot why declarer's play was wrong? With a void heart
East would surely have made a Lightner double. Also, declarer
had no re-entry for a second play on hearts – had West held
♡ J 10 x x he might have thought of splitting his honours.

5. Out of Thin Air

Italy met Indonesia in one semi-final of the 1975 World Championship. On an early board the East players, vulnerable against not, picked up:

♠ K 2
♡ A 6 5 2
♢ A 10
♣ Q 8 6 5 2

Both were playing a strong-club system and had to open one diamond on this type of hand. The auction developed like this:

SOUTH	WEST	NORTH	EAST
–		–	1♢
3♠	Dble	Pass	?

Partner's double is negative, meaning 'I have enough points to bid but no good bid to make'. His hand is likely to be flat, no doubt including four cards in hearts, the unbid major.

What actions are possible now, do you think? You can pass, if you think you can pick up some sort of penalty and that game your way is uncertain. You might introduce your club suit or you could bid game, either in hearts or no-trumps. That seems to complete the list:

(1) Pass   (2) 3NT   (3) 4♣   (4) 4♡

(No need to think 'This one's not for me,' if you don't play a one-club system. The problem would be much the same if you were playing Acol or Standard American and a three-spade overcall followed your one club opening.)

East–West Game
Dealer East

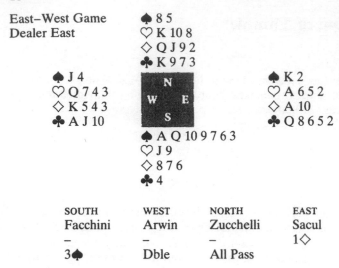

```
                    ♠ 8 5
                    ♡ K 10 8
                    ◇ Q J 9 2
                    ♣ K 9 7 3
    ♠ J 4                              ♠ K 2
    ♡ Q 7 4 3          N               ♡ A 6 5 2
    ◇ K 5 4 3      W       E           ◇ A 10
    ♣ A J 10           S               ♣ Q 8 6 5 2
                    ♠ A Q 10 9 7 6 3
                    ♡ J 9
                    ◇ 8 7 6
                    ♣ 4
```

SOUTH	WEST	NORTH	EAST
Facchini	Arwin	Zucchelli	Sacul
–	–	–	1◇
3♠	Dble	All Pass	

Denny Sacul took what appeared to be an unusual view, passing out his partner's double for penalties. The decision turned out to be inspired. West led a low heart to the 8 and ace, declarer unblocking the jack. Ace and another diamond led to a diamond ruff and Sacul then crossed to partner's ♣A for a further diamond lead. He ruffed this with the king, promoting his partner's ♠J for a second undertrick. 300 to the Indonesians.

At the other table Garozzo (East) rebid a more orthodox four hearts. After a club lead he was two down and the Indonesian master, Sacul, had conjured 11 IMPs from thin air.

The decision to leave in the double was borderline here, but most players leave in such doubles far too rarely. When your hand is flat it is often easier to take five or six tricks in defence than to struggle for ten on a 4–4 fit when the suits may break poorly. We rather admire the Indonesian's pass and – perhaps swayed by the result, we admit – give it the top marks:

Pass–5,   3NT–1,   4♣–2,   4♡–3

At both tables of the ot ot semi-final the auction started 1♣–3♠–Dble. Svarc (for France) and Eisenberg (for USA) both rebid four hearts, duplicating Garozzo's result.

6. Lesser Gamble

Five teams were involved in the 1983 North American Bermuda Bowl Trials. Warren Rosner, a member of the winning team in the Vanderbilt that year, held the following hand in a match against the Canadian team:

♠ 8
♡ A 4 3
♢ J 7 5
♣ K Q 9 8 5 4

The score was Game All and his partner opened one club, which might either be natural or a prepared bid on a weak no-trump hand. The next player overcalled three diamonds, leaving him with a tricky decision.

SOUTH	WEST	NORTH	EAST
1♣	3♢	?	–

Two obvious candidates for our list are raises to either four or five clubs. Some players might resort to a negative double, hoping that something useful would happen. A final possibility is 3NT, despite the lack of a diamond stop. It would be eccentric of us to extend the list any further. Which of the following do you like best?

(1) Dble   (2) 3NT   (3) 4♣   (4) 5♣

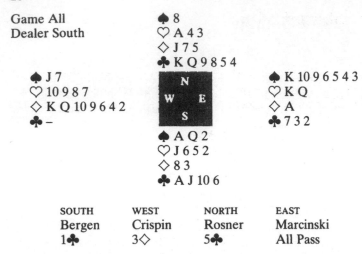

Game All
Dealer South

♠ 8
♡ A 4 3
♢ J 7 5
♣ K Q 9 8 5 4

♠ J 7
♡ 10 9 8 7
♢ K Q 10 9 6 4 2
♣ —

♠ K 10 9 6 5 4 3
♡ K Q
♢ A
♣ 7 3 2

♠ A Q 2
♡ J 6 5 2
♢ 8 3
♣ A J 10 6

SOUTH	WEST	NORTH	EAST
Bergen	Crispin	Rosner	Marcinski
1♣	3♢	5♣	All Pass

Rosner opted for five clubs. You don't fancy that contract? West led ♢K, overtaken by East's ace. Declarer won the trump return and made the imaginative play of a diamond. His idea was to tempt the defenders to ruff out dummy's useless ♢J, meanwhile leaving the squeeze threats in the majors intact.

West duly won the second diamond and returned a third round, ruffed and overruffed. When dummy's trumps were run East was squeezed and had to surrender an eleventh trick.

3NT is cold, as you see, owing to the blockage in diamonds. It seems to us that a bid of 3NT was well worth North's consideration. Holding a suit headed by the A K Q, players seldom intervene with a bid such as three diamonds; they don't want to shut their partners out of the auction. And if the diamonds cannot be run, nine tricks are almost assured.

Various favourable situations are possible apart from a blockage. South might hold a diamond honour (single queen would suffice), or he might hold three small with a void in the opening leader's hand! Those who think bidding 3NT is too dangerous may perhaps be underestimating the alternative risk – that partner won't have enough to make five clubs.

A negative double is unlikely to lead anywhere. We make it:

Double–1,   3NT–5,   4♣–2,   5♣–3

7.   Sharp End

Various problems arose on this deal from the last qualifying round of the 1983 Bermuda Bowl. Playing against New Zealand, the East player for USA 2 held:

♠ A Q 10 3
♡ 8 7 2
♢ –
♣ Q J 9 8 7 3

East–West were vulnerable and the auction began:

SOUTH	WEST	NORTH	EAST
–	–	Pass	Pass
3♢	Dble	3NT	?

Action of some kind is required, but it is difficult to express the type. Had North passed, you would be nervous of responding just four clubs on a hand of this playing strength. Now, though, it will be a free bid and must come into the reckoning. If you cannot contemplate stopping short of game, then the choices are to cue-bid four diamonds, or to bid game in either spades or clubs.

These are the possibilities:

(1) 4♣   (2) 4♢   (3) 4♣   (4) 5♣

East–West Game
Dealer North

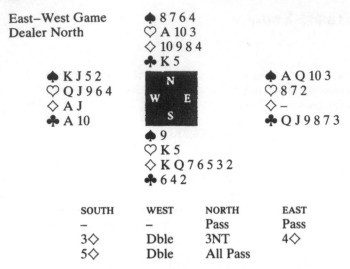

```
                  ♠ 8 7 6 4
                  ♡ A 10 3
                  ♢ 10 9 8 4
                  ♣ K 5
♠ K J 5 2                        ♠ A Q 10 3
♡ Q J 9 6 4                      ♡ 8 7 2
♢ A J                            ♢ –
♣ A 10                           ♣ Q J 9 8 7 3
                  ♠ 9
                  ♡ K 5
                  ♢ K Q 7 6 5 3 2
                  ♣ 6 4 2
```

SOUTH	WEST	NORTH	EAST
–	–	Pass	Pass
3♢	Dble	3NT	4♢
5♢	Dble	All Pass	

East's cue-bid was not a perfect solution because if West were to respond four hearts, this might well be on a four-card suit. Four diamonds is better than four spades, though, because you can continue with four spades over partner's likely four hearts, offering him a choice of the black suits.

Even opposite the respectable hand that West holds, no game is secure. Call us conservative, but we reckon that four clubs is enough on East's hand. With some doubt, admittedly, we make it:

4♣–5,   4♢–4,   4♠–3,   5♣–2

Wignall, the New Zealand South, had no very good reason to bid five diamonds over East's four diamonds. He was in luck when Jim Jacoby, West, led ♡Q. The spade loser went away on dummy's hearts and he made five diamonds doubled for +550.

At the other table Wold, South for USA 2, opened 4♢ and was doubled there. West began with ace and another club, won the first trump and crossed in spades for a club ruff with the ♢J. One down and a 13-IMP swing to the New Zealanders.

Has anything struck you? Declarer could have played three rounds of hearts, discarding the spade. East cannot then gain the lead to give West a club ruff – a brilliant Scissors Coup.

8. On His Own

The 1984 Olympiad saw an all-European final, France against Poland. Half-way through this encounter North, vulnerable against not, picked up these cards:

♠ A Q J 3
♡ A 6
◇ K J 9 7 6
♣ 9 5

At both tables his partner, South, opened one spade in second position and West rudely intervened with five clubs:

SOUTH	WEST	NORTH	EAST
–	–	–	Pass
1♠	5♣	?	

Had West passed you would doubtless have responded two diamonds, intending to issue a slam suggestion by jumping to four hearts over a two-spade rebid. Such delicate moves are now impossible and the options are to double five clubs, to bid five spades, or to turn a blind eye to your lack of a club control and jump to six spades. Which of these appeals to you most?

(1) Double   (2) 5♠   (3) 6♠

North–South Game
Dealer East

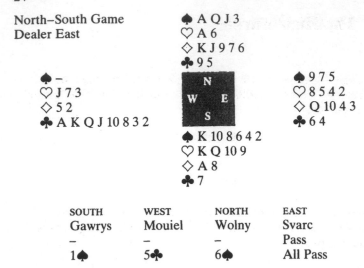

♠ A Q J 3
♡ A 6
◇ K J 9 7 6
♣ 9 5

♠ –
♡ J 7 3
◇ 5 2
♣ A K Q J 10 8 3 2

♠ 9 7 5
♡ 8 5 4 2
◇ Q 10 4 3
♣ 6 4

♠ K 10 8 6 4 2
♡ K Q 10 9
◇ A 8
♣ 7

SOUTH	WEST	NORTH	EAST
Gawrys	Mouiel	Wolny	Svarc
–	–	–	Pass
1♠	5♣	6♠	All Pass

Both Wolny and Chemla bid a bold six spades on the North cards. West's overcall suggested that South's values would be outside clubs and the odds were high that he would hold ♠K, ♡K and ◇A. The club situation was more of a concern, but if South did hold two losing clubs there was always the possibility that West would rescue the situation, sacrificing in seven clubs.

What of a five-spade bid? At adverse vulnerability partner will not expect this to be an out-and-out sacrifice. Nor will he take it as much of an invitation to bid six, though, because you might have been under pressure when you bid five. The rewards from five clubs doubled will scarcely be adequate and we mark it:

Double–1,   5♠–2,   6♠–5

At the other table Chemla's 6♠ ran round to Martens, the Polish West. Despite the fact that he had already 'bid his hand' and that Chemla might be trying to bounce him, he bid 7♣. On this occasion he was right. He went 900 down (old scoring table) against the 1430 that his colleagues achieved in six spades.

The Poles gained 11 IMPs on the board and went on to win by 236–156. The world realised, perhaps for the first time, that Poland should be ranked among the top three or four countries.

9.   The High Hurdle

In the semi-finals of the 1985 Bermuda Bowl Brazil faced the USA. Sergio Barbosa, sitting North for Brazil at one table, picked up these cards:

♠ K Q J 8 7
♡ A
♢ 7 5 3
♣ 7 4 3 2

Vulnerable against not, he heard his partner open a strong (Precision) club. The next player intervened with three hearts and the bidding proceeded:

SOUTH	WEST	NORTH	EAST
1♣ (1)	3♡	3♠ (2)	5♡
Dble	Pass	?	

(1) Precision Club, 16 points upwards.
(2) Natural, 8 points upwards.

Partner's double suggests that he does not care much for your spades. Still, your suit is good and will play opposite such as Ax. Partner must have length in at least one of the minors; perhaps six clubs from you would strike a fit. Another possibility is 5NT. In auctions where a fit is yet to be found this carries the meaning 'pick a slam, partner'.

The penalty from five hearts doubled is likely to lie somewhere between the value of a game and a slam your way. If no slam is possible it may be best to accept the pickings from that contract.

We seem to have covered all the bases. You may take your pick from these options:

(1) Pass   (2) 5♠   (3) 5NT   (4) 6♣   (5) 6♠

North–South Game
Dealer South

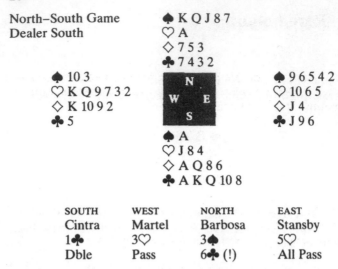

```
                    ♠ K Q J 8 7
                    ♡ A
                    ♢ 7 5 3
                    ♣ 7 4 3 2
  ♠ 10 3                              ♠ 9 6 5 4 2
  ♡ K Q 9 7 3 2                       ♡ 10 6 5
  ♢ K 10 9 2                          ♢ J 4
  ♣ 5                                 ♣ J 9 6
                    ♠ A
                    ♡ J 8 4
                    ♢ A Q 8 6
                    ♣ A K Q 10 8
```

SOUTH	WEST	NORTH	EAST
Cintra	Martel	Barbosa	Stansby
1♣	3♡	3♠	5♡
Dble	Pass	6♣ (!)	All Pass

Barbosa judged that the opponents were likely to hold the missing honours in hearts and that partner would therefore be packed in the minors. Introducing a new suit at the six level on just four to the seven is something of a novelty. At the score, however, there is always the extra chance that when you have made the wrong decision an opponent will sacrifice.

Six clubs was very much the right decision. Cintra must have been so shocked when he heard the bid that he forgot to raise to the grand. Just as well, since the bad breaks forced him to attempt a diamond finesse for the thirteenth trick.

If 5NT is available, in the sense we described it, this is a clear winner (no doubt the Brazilians had some other use for the bid). We mark it:

Pass–2,   5♠–1,   5NT–5,   6♣–3,   6♠–0

Does anything else strike you? Cintra's double of five hearts seems wrong to us. Holding three hearts, and with the opponents bidding to the five level in that suit, he could be confident of at most a singleton heart opposite. With his 20 points facing at least 8 in partner's hand, surely six clubs was a more reasonable gamble from the South hand than it was from North's.

10. Rare Failure

Towards the end of the 1993 Olympiad final between France and USA the two North players were faced with the same decision on a competitive deal. At Love All they held:

♠ Q 7 3
♡ 10 8 2
◇ A Q 10 8
♣ A 10 4

There was an opening of one heart to their left and partner overcalled two clubs. A pre-emptive jump to four hearts by right-hand opponent now caused something of a problem:

SOUTH	WEST	NORTH	EAST
–	–	–	1♡
2♣	4♡	?	

One possibility is to pass. Another is to double, showing general values. The third option is to raise partner's clubs to the five level. Which of these appeals to you most?

(1) Pass   (2) Dble   (3) 5♣

Love All   ♠ Q 7 3
Dealer East   ♡ 10 8 2
                   ◇ A Q 10 8
                   ♣ A 10 4

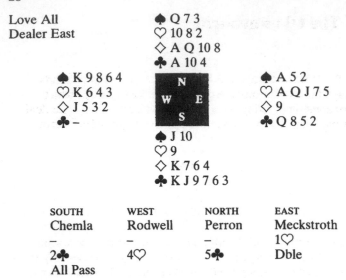

♠ K 9 8 6 4   ♠ A 5 2
♡ K 6 4 3   ♡ A Q J 7 5
◇ J 5 3 2   ◇ 9
♣ –   ♣ Q 8 5 2

                  ♠ J 10
                  ♡ 9
                  ◇ K 7 6 4
                  ♣ K J 9 7 6 3

SOUTH	WEST	NORTH	EAST
Chemla	Rodwell	Perron	Meckstroth
–	–	–	1♡
2♣	4♡	5♣	Dble
All Pass			

Perron opted for five clubs, which was doubled by East. When
Chemla picked up the trump queen, this was only one down
against a making four hearts.

What led North to this fine decision? He knew from the
opponents' auction that his partner would hold at most one heart.
South was likely to score six club tricks and if there were two or
three losers in spades and diamonds the opponents would surely
succeed in four hearts. We make five clubs a clear winner and
award these marks:

Pass–1,   Dble–1,   5♣–5

At the other table Rosenberg, North for the USA, preferred to
double four hearts. A poor call from a very fine player, it seems
to us. Declarer played safely for ten tricks, after a trump lead,
and that was +590 to France.

You may have noted that the 3–2 spade break would allow
East–West to make *eleven* tricks in hearts. If we look back to the
auction at the first table, should Meckstroth perhaps have bid five
hearts rather than double five clubs? He could place his partner
with a void club and there was no reason to expect more than two
losers in spades and diamonds combined.

11.   The Old Favourite

During the 1993 world championships in Chile the same hands were played in the Bermuda Bowl and the Venice Cup, which made for some interesting comparisons. At Love All on one deal the German star, Sabine Zenkel, held these cards in the North seat:

♠ K Q 10 8 6 2
♡ K 3 2
♢ 10 8 5 4
♣ –

There was a three-club opening on her left, followed by a take-out double from her partner, Daniela von Arnim. Zenkel might have responded four spades but she chose instead to show her strength with a cue-bid of four clubs. The bidding continued like this:

SOUTH	WEST	NORTH	EAST
–	–	–	3♣
Dble	Pass	4♣	Pass
4♢	Pass	?	

What action do you favour now? You could introduce your spades, at the four or five level, or raise to five diamonds. If you feel more optimistic than that, you might bid Blackwood or perhaps cue bid five clubs. These seem to be the main options:

(1) 4♠   (2) 4NT   (3) 5♣   (4) 5♢   (5) 5♠

Love All
Dealer East

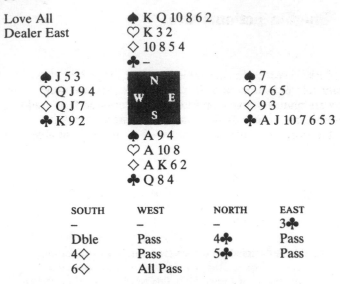

♠ K Q 10 8 6 2
♡ K 3 2
◇ 10 8 5 4
♣ –

♠ J 5 3
♡ Q J 9 4
◇ Q J 7
♣ K 9 2

♠ 7
♡ 7 6 5
◇ 9 3
♣ A J 10 7 6 5 3

♠ A 9 4
♡ A 10 8
◇ A K 6 2
♣ Q 8 4

SOUTH	WEST	NORTH	EAST
–	–	–	3♣
Dble	Pass	4♣	Pass
4◇	Pass	5♣	Pass
6◇	All Pass		

West led ♣2 and with the diamonds breaking 3–2 the play presented no problems. Declarer ruffed, cashed two diamonds, then played on spades, conceding just a trump trick. At the other table South played in five spades, just made, so there was a big swing to the German team.

As for North's bid in response to South's four diamonds, we have an awful feeling that at this point we might have bid four spades rather than five clubs. In deference to Zenkel's successful choice we make it:

4♠–4,   4NT–0,   5♣–5,   5◇–2,   5♠–1

In the Bermuda Bowl, meanwhile, both the Norwegian and the Dutch South players bid 3NT over three clubs, finishing in four spades. The critics seemed to approve of South's 3NT, in preference to a double, but of course a double by South does not exclude an eventual 3NT.

The interesting point about the deal is the support it lends to the presumption that the 4–4 fit (diamonds) will often bring in an extra trick when compared with 9-card fit elsewhere (spades). In a spade contract there is no way to dispose of the heart loser; in diamonds, the spade side-suit provides a discard.

12. The Collection Plate

Sabine Zenkel, heroine of the preceding deal, played an important role in this one too. In 1994, once again, the same boards were played in two world finals, the Bermuda Bowl and the Venice Cup. As one might expect, there were four quite different auctions on a deal where East–West were vulnerable and South held:

♠ –
♡ 9
♢ A J 10 9 6
♣ A K Q 10 6 4 3

When Zenkel held this fine two-suiter, the bidding began:

SOUTH	WEST	NORTH	EAST
–	2♢ (1)	Pass	Pass
?			

(1) Weak two-bid, six diamonds and 6–10 points.

The possibilities are to pass, hoping to collect a few 100s, to bid some number of clubs, or even to make a natural bid in no-trumps, trusting partner to stop the major suits. These are the possibilities:

(1) Pass   (2) 3♣   (3) 3NT   (4) 4♣   (5) 5♣

East–West Game
Dealer West

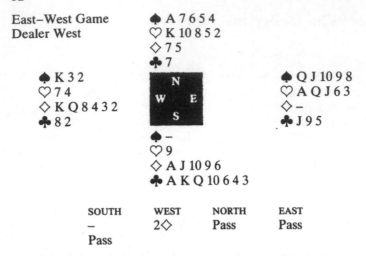

```
                    ♠ A 7 6 5 4
                    ♡ K 10 8 5 2
                    ♢ 7 5
                    ♣ 7
♠ K 3 2                                    ♠ Q J 10 9 8
♡ 7 4               N                      ♡ A Q J 6 3
♢ K Q 8 4 3 2     W   E                    ♢ –
♣ 8 2               S                      ♣ J 9 5
                    ♠ –
                    ♡ 9
                    ♢ A J 10 9 6
                    ♣ A K Q 10 6 4 3
```

SOUTH	WEST	NORTH	EAST
–	2♢	Pass	Pass
Pass			

Zenkel's Pass on the South cards was an intelligent move, likely to bring in 400 or so. In fact, the American West made a muddle of the play. She was overruffed on the third round of clubs and subsequently led a high diamond from hand, managing to go six down.

A good alternative on the South cards is an eccentric-looking 3NT! You have a probable eight tricks yourself and dummy will surely provide some cover in the majors. Game in clubs is a less likely target, requiring more help from the dummy than you would need to make 3NT. We like 3NT as much as a Pass and award these marks:

Pass–5,   3♣–0,   3NT–5,   4♣–2,   5♣–3

At the other table of this match South was one down in five clubs, Germany picking up a swing of 11 IMPs.

In the Bermuda Bowl the Norwegian South promoted himself into six clubs, down two. Finally, after a third-in-hand one spade by the Norwegian East, the Dutch South bid 2NT to announce his minor two-suiter. He played there, making nine tricks, and that was 6 IMPs to the Netherlands.

PART II   THE CONSTRUCTIVE AUCTION

In this section we consider auctions where the opponents are
mercifully silent. The top players work hard on their bidding
systems and you won't find them far off the mark on the majority
of these deals.

13.   Neither Side Shone

It is popularly held that the bidding of years ago may have been
agricultural but that the card-play of the top stars was as good as
today. If this is true you would hardly guess it from the
performances of the two declarers on the present deal. It comes
from the first Bermuda Bowl, played in 1950.

Howard Schenken sat South for the USA, facing a combined
Sweden–Iceland team, and picked up these cards at Love All:

> ♠ A Q J 4
> ♡ 10 7
> ♢ Q J 10 4 3
> ♣ Q 8

This was the start to the auction:

SOUTH	WEST	NORTH	EAST
Schenken	Thorfinnson	Crawford	Gudmundson
–	Pass	1♡	Pass
2♢	Pass	3♣	Pass
3NT	Pass	4♢	Pass
?			

Partner is suggesting a diamond slam. If you are not
enthusiastic you may sign off, either in 4NT or in five diamonds.
Should you rate your hand more highly you can cue-bid four
spades or simply leap to six diamonds. These are the options:

(1) 4♠   (2) 4NT   (3) 5♢   (4) 6♣

Love all
Dealer West

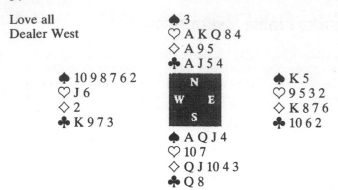

```
                    ♠ 3
                    ♡ A K Q 8 4
                    ◇ A 9 5
                    ♣ A J 5 4
♠ 10 9 8 7 6 2              ♠ K 5
♡ J 6          N           ♡ 9 5 3 2
◇ 2        W     E         ◇ K 8 7 6
♣ K 9 7 3      S           ♣ 10 6 2
                    ♠ A Q J 4
                    ♡ 10 7
                    ◇ Q J 10 4 3
                    ♣ Q 8
```

SOUTH	WEST	NORTH	EAST
Schenken	Thorfinnson	Crawford	Gudmundson
–	Pass	1♡	Pass
2◇	Pass	3♣	Pass
3NT	Pass	4◇	Pass
4NT	All Pass		

Evidently, Schenken was influenced by the duplication of values in spades. Partner could easily hold ♡ A K and ♣ A K and a top diamond, however, giving an easy six diamonds. We mark it:

$$4♠–5, \quad 4NT–1, \quad 5◇–1, \quad 6◇–4$$

West led ♣10 to the king and ace. Schenken could have played on hearts, reaching his spade tricks with a diamond. He ran ◇Q instead, East holding up. He could still have cashed ♠ Q J and run ♣Q into the safe hand. No, he played a diamond to the ace and four rounds of hearts. The defenders could now have end-played the dummy, scoring two clubs, a diamond and a heart. West had thrown a club, however, and declarer survived.

In the replay Werner (North) landed in five hearts! After ♣J, ♣A, and a club ruff, he then ran ◇Q to the king, West ruffing the diamond return. Werner ruffed a fourth club with dummy's ♡10, East throwing a spade. When he cashed ♠A and ruffed a spade with the 8, East overruffed. West ruffed a second diamond and a spade now promoted a trick for East's ♡ 5 3 2. Three down! Declarer could have succeeded by simply drawing trumps and playing on diamonds.

14. Unfortunate Assumption

In an early Camrose match between England and Scotland, Skinner sat South for Scotland and picked up these cards:

♠ A Q 8 6 2
♡ A J
♢ K 9 6 5
♣ 9 6

With the opponents vulnerable, he opened one spade and the bidding continued:

SOUTH	WEST	NORTH	EAST
1♠	Pass	3♢	Pass
4♢	Pass	4♠	Pass
?			

Only 14 points but a good fit for partner and three or four important cards. Pass will be on our list, but if you do decide to look for a slam what is the best next move?

One possibility is Blackwood (not Roman Key-Card in those days, you understand). If you feel you should direct partner's attention to the club weakness you could cue-bid the ace of hearts instead. Finally, you could leap to six spades – aiming to give West no help with his opening lead.

There is little merit in five diamonds or an indeterminate five spades, so this is our list:

(1) Pass   (2) 4NT   (3) 5♡   (4) 6♠

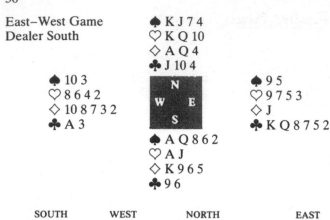

East–West Game   ♠ K J 7 4
Dealer South   ♡ K Q 10
                    ◇ A Q 4
                    ♣ J 10 4

♠ 10 3   ♠ 9 5
♡ 8 6 4 2   ♡ 9 7 5 3
◇ 10 8 7 3 2   ◇ J
♣ A 3   ♣ K Q 8 7 5 2

                    ♠ A Q 8 6 2
                    ♡ A J
                    ◇ K 9 6 5
                    ♣ 9 6

SOUTH	WEST	NORTH	EAST
Skinner	J. Tarlo	Mrs Davidson	Rockfelt
1♠	Pass	3◇	Pass
4◇	Pass	4♠	Pass
6♠	All Pass		

The Scottish South leapt gaily (if one is allowed to use that word nowadays) to 6♠. Joel Tarlo, West, who held five diamonds and had heard both opponents bid the suit, placed his partner with a void. He led ◇2, his lowest diamond, suggesting a club return; a second ruff would then put the contract two down.

A small flaw in this plan was exposed when East followed to the first diamond. Declarer drew one round of trumps and promptly faced his cards, claiming twelve tricks.

Tarlo might have attached more weight to the lack of a Lightner double from his partner. In any case, two down is worth little more than one down. It can hardly be wrong to begin with ♣A, planning to switch to diamonds at trick 2. After such a start East would signal emphatically for a club continuation.

Despite the success of South's tactics, his best continuation must be five hearts, pin-pointing the weakness in clubs. North would then close the shop at five spades. A pass of four spades would be too timid and Blackwood unsound when holding two losing clubs. We see it like this:

Pass–1,   4NT–1,   5♡–5,   6♠–3

15.   Rather Neat

In the final of the Whitelaw Cup, the English women's championship, South opened a conventional two clubs and her partner held:

♠ 3
♡ J 7 6 2
♢ A J 10 7 3
♣ Q 5 3

She made the positive response of three diamonds – borderline on her cards, but reasonable enough because over the expected three spades from partner 3NT would give a fair picture of the values held. The bidding continued:

SOUTH	WEST	NORTH	EAST
2♣	Pass	3♢	Pass
3♠	Pass	3NT	Pass
4♣	Pass	?	

What now? Partner will not necessarily hold five clubs but the hand might play well in a 4–3 fit anyway. If raising the clubs to the five or six level does not appeal, you can mark time with four diamonds, or bid a natural 4NT. These are the options:

(1) 4♢   (2) 4NT   (3) 5♣   (4) 6♣

East–West Game
Dealer South

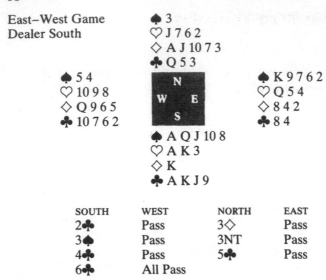

```
                       ♠ 3
                       ♡ J 7 6 2
                       ◇ A J 10 7 3
                       ♣ Q 5 3
♠ 5 4                                    ♠ K 9 7 6 2
♡ 10 9 8                                 ♡ Q 5 4
◇ Q 9 6 5              N                  ◇ 8 4 2
♣ 10 7 6 2         W       E              ♣ 8 4
                       S
                       ♠ A Q J 10 8
                       ♡ A K 3
                       ◇ K
                       ♣ A K J 9
```

SOUTH	WEST	NORTH	EAST
2♣	Pass	3◇	Pass
3♠	Pass	3NT	Pass
4♣	Pass	5♣	Pass
6♣	All Pass		

This was good bidding by the Yorkshire partnership of Rene
Corwen (South) and Rita Oldroyd. Five clubs seems exactly right.
To jump to six clubs would be too much on the North hand, since
the singleton spade (when holding only three trumps) is scarcely
an asset. We mark it:

$$4◇–2, \quad 4NT–1, \quad 5♣–5, \quad 6♣–2$$

West led ♡10 against six clubs. South won, cashed the ace of
spades, and ran the queen, losing to the king. East returned a
trump now and declarer won in hand, cashed the king of
diamonds, and crossed to dummy with the trump queen. She
discarded a heart on the ace of diamonds, then drew trumps,
relying on a spade break. When that failed she was one down.

No-one at the time noticed a rather neat alternative. After
winning the first trick with the ace of hearts South should run a
middle spade, losing to the king. She can then win the trump
return, cash the diamond king and ruff ♠8. This play rescues the
contract when the spades are 5–2.

16. Not Born Yesterday

Fritzi Gordon, whose partnership with Rixi Markus swept all before it, picked up this freak hand during the Ladies Trials of 1958:

> ♠ A J 10 8 7 6 5 4 2
> ♡ A 9 5
> ♢ 10
> ♣ –

With the score at Love All, her partner opened a 12–14 1NT and the next player passed.

SOUTH	WEST	NORTH	EAST
–	–	1NT	Pass
?			

What move is most appropriate now, do you think? You could start with a forcing three spades or perhaps a Gerber four clubs, asking for aces. If you prefer to determine the matter at a stroke you could bid a direct four spades or six spades. If those bids are on our list, then we should find a place for five spades as well. Which of these would catch your eye?

(1) 3♠   (2) 4♣ (Gerber)   (3) 4♠   (4) 5♠   (5) 6♠

Love all   ♠ Q 9
Dealer North   ♡ Q 10 7 4
                 ◇ A 9 7 6
                 ♣ A Q 7

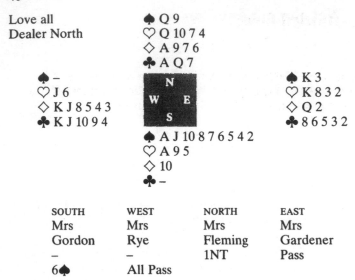

♠ –   ♠ K 3
♡ J 6   ♡ K 8 3 2
◇ K J 8 5 4 3   ◇ Q 2
♣ K J 10 9 4   ♣ 8 6 5 3 2

                   ♠ A J 10 8 7 6 5 4 2
                   ♡ A 9 5
                   ◇ 10
                   ♣ –

SOUTH	WEST	NORTH	EAST
Mrs	Mrs	Mrs	Mrs
Gordon	Rye	Fleming	Gardener
–	–	1NT	Pass
6♠	All Pass		

As anyone who knew her would predict, Fritzi made the practical, rubber-bridge response of 6♠. Some players would shake their heads at this but if you bid more descriptively – jumping in spades, then showing your club control, you are less likely to receive a favourable opening lead (for example, a club when partner has the ace and you can throw your diamond loser). Asking for aces, here via Gerber, is rarely profitable when you have a void. We like Fritzi's response best and mark it:

      3♠–2,   4♣–0,   4♠–0,   5♠–1,   6♠–5

Despite Fritzi's unrevealing leap West did find the only safe lead – a diamond. (It was sensible to choose her longest suit). Declarer won in the dummy and called for the trump queen. Mrs Gardener, not born yesterday, produced a cool 3 and Fritzi rose with the ace. A heart had to be lost, so that was one down.

A tiny, almost invisible, safety play would have won the day. If declarer is not planning to finesse in trumps it costs her nothing to ruff a diamond at trick 2. Then ace and another trump leaves East on play. If trumps are 1–1, of course, the queen of trumps will provide an entry to throw one heart loser on ♣A.

17. Bowled Over

The final of the 1960 Hubert Phillips Bowl (the British Mixed Teams Knock-Out) saw Boris Schapiro's team facing that of Rixi Markus. Early in the match the South players held:

♠ A Q 3
♡ Q J 10 8 4
♦ 9 8 7 6 3
♣ –

North–South were vulnerable and at the table where Claude Rodrigue sat South, this was the start to the auction:

SOUTH	WEST	NORTH	EAST
Rodrigue	Konstam	Dodds	Schapiro
–	–	1♦	Pass
1♡	Pass	3♡	Pass
?			

There are several possibilities now. If you reckon that the game level is high enough you can bid four hearts. Another possibility is to cue-bid three spades, or perhaps jump to five clubs to show the club void. If a direct blast to six is more your style, you will still have to judge which suit should become trumps.

These are the options:

(1) 3♠   (2) 4♡   (3) 5♣   (4) 6♦   (5) 6♡

Love all · · · · · · · · · · · · · ♠ 10 4 2
Dealer North · · · · · · · · · · ♡ A K 6
· ◇ A Q 4 2
· ♣ K 7 3

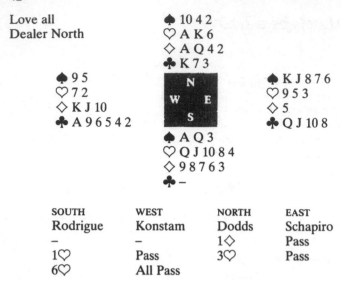

♠ 9 5
♡ 7 2
◇ K J 10
♣ A 9 6 5 4 2

♠ K J 8 7 6
♡ 9 5 3
◇ 5
♣ Q J 10 8

· ♠ A Q 3
· ♡ Q J 10 8 4
· ◇ 9 8 7 6 3
· ♣ –

SOUTH	WEST	NORTH	EAST
Rodrigue	Konstam	Dodds	Schapiro
–	–	1◇	Pass
1♡	Pass	3♡	Pass
6♡	All Pass		

If ever there was a hand where a direct jump to six was justified, this seems to be it. Which suit should you play in? Rodrigue was keen to play in hearts, to protect his spades from the opening lead. This makes good sense, although if you play in diamonds and the defenders do not find a spade lead, your heart suit may provide a discard from partner's hand. We mark it:

> 3♠–2, · · · · 4♡–1, · · · · 5♣–1, · · · · 6◇–4, · · · · 6♡–5

When West led ♠9 against six hearts it was apparent that the spade king was onside and that six diamonds would have been a better proposition. Rodrigue won with the queen, drew trumps in three rounds and led ◇9 to the queen. He continued with ◇A, dropping the 8 from hand.

The stage was now set. Had declarer removed West's last spade and continued with ◇7, West would have been forced to play on clubs, setting up ♣K for a spade discard. (The ◇3 to the 4 would provide the entry). Rodrigue played the diamonds correctly but forgot to extract West's spade. One down.

At the other table North opened 1◇ and East overcalled 1♠. When South raised his partner to 5◇, West's double must have seemed gilt-edged. Unlucky to find that 12 tricks were cold . . .

18.   'Luck be a Lady'

The 1964 final of the Whitelaw Cup, the English Women's Championship, was as dramatic as any script-writer could devise. The team captained by Honor Rye (later Honor Flint) had always been ahead of Phyllis Williams, but after 63 boards, with one to play, the margin was only 8 IMPs.

At this stage South picked up:

♠ Q 10 8 7 5 4
♡ A K 5
♢ A K Q 6
♣ –

The bidding began:

SOUTH	WEST	NORTH	EAST
1♠	Pass	1NT	Pass
3♢	Pass	3♠	Pass
?			

If the slam bonus still beckons there are various possibilities. You could cue-bid four clubs, or perhaps jump to five clubs to indicate the void. You might instead cue-bid the ace of hearts, intending to cue-bid in clubs later. A further option is to jump to five spades, perhaps indicating to partner that all suits are under control but some help is needed in trumps.

If you don't regard the slam prospects too highly, you could sign off in four spades. These are the options:

(1) 4♣   (2) 4♡   (3) 4♠   (4) 5♣   (5) 5♠

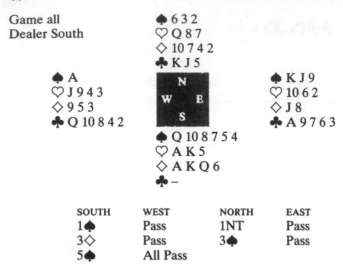

Game all   ♠ 6 3 2
Dealer South   ♡ Q 8 7
                 ◇ 10 7 4 2
                 ♣ K J 5

♠ A   ♠ K J 9
♡ J 9 4 3   ♡ 10 6 2
◇ 9 5 3   ◇ J 8
♣ Q 10 8 4 2   ♣ A 9 7 6 3

                 ♠ Q 10 8 7 5 4
                 ♡ A K 5
                 ◇ A K Q 6
                 ♣ −

SOUTH	WEST	NORTH	EAST
1♠	Pass	1NT	Pass
3◇	Pass	3♠	Pass
5♠	All Pass		

One doesn't know to what extent South was influenced by the state of the match. Disregarding that, a slam try of four clubs or four hearts is reasonable, and so is a simple four spades. A slam try above game level is not altogether sound, since there is a danger of duplication in clubs. We suggest:

4♣–5,   4♡–5,   4♠–4,   5♣–2,   5♠–1

West led a low club to the jack and ace, South ruffing. Declarer crossed to ♡Q and led a low spade to the 10 and ace. Two more trump tricks had to be lost and she was now one down, against 650 at the other table. That was 13 IMPs away, and the match, to opponents who had taken the lead for the first time.

After ruffing the club lead in five spades South has a tricky problem. Except in very unlikely circumstances you will always succeed if trumps are 2–2. Low from hand is best when West has a singleton ace or king, as you will be able to cross to dummy for the next lead. A heart to dummy, then a spade to the queen, wins when either defender holds a singleton jack; so does the queen of spades from hand.

The one play that can never gain is the one adopted by the declarer – heart to dummy and a finesse of ♠10. Unlucky!

19. Bull's-Eye

The final of the 1965 World Championship was fought between Italy and USA. On one board, at Love All, North held:

♠ K 8 2
♡ K Q 8 6 5 3
♦ J 7
♣ Q 8

At both tables the auction started like this:

SOUTH	WEST	NORTH	EAST
1♣	Pass	1♡	Pass
1♠	Pass	?	

There are several possibilities now. You could bid a conservative two hearts, or perhaps two spades. If the bid is not forcing in your system, you might bid three hearts. A final possibility is to make an artificial bid in the fourth suit – two diamonds. Over to you.

(1) 2♦   (2) 2♡   (3) 2♠   (4) 3♡

Love all
Dealer South

      ♠ K 8 2
      ♡ K Q 8 6 5 3
      ◇ J 7
      ♣ Q 8

♠ 10 7 4   ♠ 9 5 3
♡ J 4   ♡ 10 9 2
◇ A 4 3   ◇ K 10 9 5 2
♣ A 10 9 6 3   ♣ K 7

      ♠ A Q J 6
      ♡ A 7
      ◇ Q 8 6
      ♣ J 5 4 2

SOUTH	WEST	NORTH	EAST
D'Alelio	Leventrit	Pabis-Ticci	Schenken
1♣	Pass	1♡	Pass
1♠	Pass	3♡	Pass
3NT	All Pass		

D'Alelio and Pabis-Ticci scored a bull's-eye with this simple auction. The defenders played three rounds of clubs and declarer could claim eleven tricks when the hearts broke 3–2.

At the other table Petterson, the American North, was hampered by the fact that three hearts on the second round would be forcing. It was perhaps the main difference between US and European bidding systems at that time that the Americans treated many more sequences as forcing. Deciding to keep something in reserve, Petterson rebid just two hearts. This ended the auction and the Italians picked up a game swing.

Some three decades later, most Americans would treat a jump to three hearts as non-forcing. This makes good sense because whenever you hold a stronger hand you can inject a fourth-suit bid (here two diamonds); a subsequent three-heart bid will then be forcing.

On that understanding, it would be wrong to bid two diamonds on the present hand. Three hearts is clearly best, despite the moderate quality of the suit, and we mark it:

     2◇–1,   2♡–2,   2♠–2,   3♡–5

20.   Even the Mighty

Norway faced Italy at an early stage of the 1970 Bermuda Bowl and the two North players picked up this hand:

♠ Q 10
♡ K Q J 10 6 3
♢ A Q 4 2
♣ 3

For the moment we will consider the hand from the Norwegian North's point of view. He opened one heart and heard his partner respond two spades. His rebid of three hearts was certainly more sensible than introducing the diamonds and partner now seemed to lose patience with the auction, which continued:

SOUTH	WEST	NORTH	EAST
–	–	1♡	Pass
2♠	Pass	3♡	Pass
6NT	Pass	?	

The question is . . . do your extra values entitle you to bid a grand? If so, you have the option of bidding it in hearts or no-trumps. Only three choices this time:

(1) Pass   (2) 7♡   (3) 7NT

East–West game   ♠ Q 10
Dealer North   ♡ K Q J 10 6 3
                  ◇ A Q 4 2
                  ♣ 3

♠ J 8 5 2   ♠ 6 4
♡ 9 7 5 2   N   ♡ 8 4
◇ 9   W   E   ◇ J 8 6 5 3
♣ K Q 6 4   S   ♣ 10 8 7 5

                  ♠ A K 9 7 3
                  ♡ A
                  ◇ K 10 7
                  ♣ A J 9 2

SOUTH	WEST	NORTH	EAST
Strom	Moriai	Hoie	Barbarisi
–	–	1♡	Pass
2♠	Pass	3♡	Pass
6NT	Pass	7NT	All Pass

When partner has leapt to a small slam you must consider very carefully before raising to seven. Even if you have several extra tricks for him, there may still be one unavoidable loser.

Here Hoie faced a partner who had not used Blackwood. Holding one ace himself, he could therefore be certain that partner held the other three aces. Since South would scarcely have bid 6NT with a jack-high diamond holding, he must also hold ◇K. Add the very likely ♠K and there would be thirteen tricks – six hearts, three spades, three hearts and one club. So, 7NT it had to be. We mark it:

Pass–1,   7♡–3,   7NT–5

No doubt you have now and again heard such as: 'Sorry, partner. I had a club in with my spades.' You may be surprised to hear that these words were uttered (in Italian, at any rate) on this very deal. De Ritis, the Italian South, had a small club with his spades. Over 1♡ he bid 2♠, which in his system promised much better spades than he actually held. The Italians duly reached 7♠, at which point De Ritis was horrified to notice something very peculiar about his 'two of spades'. The spade jack failed to drop and the Norsemen collected 17 IMPs.

21. Second Choice

Norway represented Europe in the 1970 world championship, held in Stockholm. They had a lucky break on this deal, as you will see in a moment. Goldman was North for the USA and picked up this hand at Game All:

♠ Q J 10 9 4
♡ Q 4
♢ K 7 3
♣ K Q 5

Playing Standard American, he opened one spade and heard his partner respond 1NT, forcing. The bidding developed like this:

SOUTH	WEST	NORTH	EAST
–	–	1♠	Pass
1NT (1)	2♣	Pass	Pass
3♠	Pass	?	

(1) Forcing.

Partner suggests a balanced hand with three-card spade support and about 10–11 points. With only 13 points yourself and no aces, a pass would normally suggest itself. The main point of interest is how the decision is affected by your well-placed club holding: K Q x over the two-club bidder.

You to speak, then. These are the choices:

(1) Pass　　(2) 3NT　　(3) 4♠

Game All   ♠ Q J 10 9 4
Dealer North   ♡ Q 4
                  ◇ K 7 3
                  ♣ K Q 5

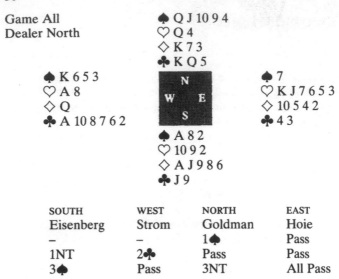

♠ K 6 5 3   ♠ 7
♡ A 8   ♡ K J 7 6 5 3
◇ Q   ◇ 10 5 4 2
♣ A 10 8 7 6 2   ♣ 4 3

                  ♠ A 8 2
                  ♡ 10 9 2
                  ◇ A J 9 8 6
                  ♣ J 9

SOUTH	WEST	NORTH	EAST
Eisenberg	Strom	Goldman	Hoie
–	–	1♠	Pass
1NT	2♣	Pass	Pass
3♠	Pass	3NT	All Pass

Goldman's decision to attempt 3NT seems an overbid to us. Even with two club stops, the lack of aces is likely to prove too much of a handicap. We mark it:

Pass–5,   3NT–3,   4♠–1

How would you expect the play to go in 3NT? Suppose West leads a club and declarer wins with dummy's king, running ♠Q next. Is there not a fair chance that West will continue clubs? Of course, he would do better to hold off the first spade, waiting for a signal from his partner.

This all proved academic at the table when Hoie led ♣4 out of turn (it was before the days of face-down leads). Declarer now had various options at his disposal and some say that you should generally accept the lead out of turn – since anyone silly enough to make such a lead is unlikely to have chosen a good one!

Eisenberg was unimpressed by his club stop, though (he couldn't see the dummy yet, remember). He prohibited a club lead and West tried his luck with ♡A. A delighted East signalled for a continuation and the defenders took the first six tricks. After a spade switch they had to come to two more and that was −400.

22. The Tide Turned

One of the most famous bridge matches of all time was the final of the 1975 World Championship, between Italy and the USA. You have probably read about the deal near the end where Belladonna landed seven clubs for the Italians with a trump holding of ♣ J 9 8 6 3 2 opposite ♣ A Q (poor Eddie Kantar held ♣ K 10 under the A Q).

At an earlier stage in this match the Italians were a massive 72 IMPs behind. The North players, with the opponents vulnerable, drew these cards from the wallet:

$$
\begin{array}{l}
\spadesuit \text{ J 7 3 2} \\
\heartsuit \text{ A Q 10} \\
\diamondsuit \text{ J 8} \\
\clubsuit \text{ A K 7 2}
\end{array}
$$

When their respective partners opened one spade they decided to go slowly with a two-club response. At the table where Pittala was North for Italy the auction developed like this:

SOUTH	WEST	NORTH	EAST
–	–	–	Pass
1♠	Pass	2♣	Pass
2♠	Pass	3♡	Pass
3NT	Pass	4♣	Pass
4NT (1)	Pass	?	

(1) Not Blackwood, but a general slam try.

Your sequence, travelling via three hearts, has suggested more values than a raise to four spades on the previous round would have done. Partner has responded to this initiative with a further move of his own over four spades.

What should you do now? If disinclined to head for a slam you could pass or sign off in five spades. If you like the look of your hand you may prefer to jump to six spades. The middle path would be to cue-bid five clubs, consulting partner further on the matter. These are the choices:

(1) Pass   (2) 5♣   (3) 5♠   (4) 6♠

East–West game
Dealer East

             ♠ J 7 3 2
             ♡ A Q 10
             ◇ J 8
             ♣ A K 7 2

♠ 9   ♠ A 6 5
♡ K 7 6 4 2   **N**   ♡ J 8
◇ 9 4 3   **W**   **E**   ◇ Q 10 7 6 5 2
♣ J 10 5 4   **S**   ♣ 8 6

             ♠ K Q 10 8 4
             ♡ 9 5 3
             ◇ A K
             ♣ Q 9 3

SOUTH	WEST	NORTH	EAST
Franco	Swanson	Pittala	Soloway
–	–	–	Pass
1♠	Pass	2♣	Pass
2♠	Pass	3♡	Pass
3NT	Pass	4♠	Pass
4NT	Pass	6♠	All Pass

Pittala, no doubt with the match score in mind, jumped to six spades. Swanson led a heart and declarer called for the queen from dummy (clearly better than the 10, since the club suit may provide a discard). When this held, he forced out the ace of trumps, East returning the heart jack to dummy's ace. Declarer now cashed his winners in spades and diamonds, squeezing West in hearts and clubs for a twelfth trick. +980 for Italy.

The slam was not a good one, as you see, requiring ♡K to be well placed in addition to some favourable disposition of the club suit. At the other table Bob Hamman judged the hand well when his partner 'came again' with 5◇ over 4♠. He signed off in 5♠, fearing that a cue-bid of 5♡ might excite partner unduly.

It was a fair gamble to attempt six spades when 72 IMPs behind. Here, we will consider the hand in isolation. We make it:

Pass–2,   5♣–3,   5♠–5,   6♠–1

At this point the tide turned in favour of the Italians. They eventually overtook their great rivals, winning by 25 IMPs.

23.   We Meet Again

Italy met North America, yet again, in the final of the 1976
Bermuda Bowl. Italy led throughout the first of the two days, but
their lead had been cut to 4 IMPs when the final board of the
second day was placed on the table. Rubin, South for North
America (if that's not confusing), picked up these cards:

♠ 4 3
♡ A 8 4
♢ K Q J 10 4
♣ J 10 8

When his partner opened one heart in the second seat he
responded two diamonds. The bidding continued like this:

SOUTH	WEST	NORTH	EAST
–	Pass	1♡	Pass
2♢	Pass	2♠	Pass
3♡	Pass	4NT	Pass
5♢	Pass	5NT	Pass
6♢	Pass	6♡	Pass
?			

Partner has taken control with Blackwood and you have shown
one ace and one king. Is his bid of six hearts the end of the
matter, would you say, or does your source of tricks in diamonds
entitle you to bid again? Certainly his 5NT bid should mean that
he holds three aces.
     If you decide to battle onwards, you could correct to 6NT or
bid a grand – in diamonds, hearts or no-trumps. These are the
possibilities:

   (1) Pass   (2) 6NT   (3) 7♢   (4) 7♡   (5) 7NT

54

East–West game
Dealer West

♠ A 10 5 2
♡ K Q J 3 2
♢ A
♣ A Q 5

♠ J 7 6		♠ K Q 9 8
♡ 7 6	N	♡ 10 9 5
♢ 8 5 3 2	W E	♢ 9 7 6
♣ K 7 6 4	S	♣ 9 3 2

♠ 4 3
♡ A 8 4
♢ K Q J 10 4
♣ J 10 8

SOUTH	WEST	NORTH	EAST
Rubin	Forquet	Soloway	Belladonna
–	Pass	1♡	Pass
2♢	Pass	2♠	Pass
3♡	Pass	4NT	Pass
5♢	Pass	5NT	Pass
6♢	Pass	6♡	Pass
7♢	Pass	7NT	All Pass

Soloway's 5NT confirmed that the partnership held all four
aces. The hearts were likely to be solid, so Rubin could visualise
five tricks in each red suit and two aces – a total of twelve. A
nondescript 4–5–2–2 hand of 18 points would scarcely justify
North's rush to Blackwood, so the odds were high that he held a
sixth heart, or some other extra value. Rubin bid seven diamonds
(better than 7NT when partner has ♡ K Q x x x and the heart suit
needs to be ruffed good) and Soloway corrected to 7NT.

As it turned out, the contract depended on a club finesse. When
this succeeded the Americans gained 11 IMPs, the Italians having
stopped in six. After taking the lead at a psychologically
important moment, the US team went on to win by 34 IMPs.

To the marking. When partner bids 5NT, asking for kings, you
are invited to proceed to a grand if you have an unidentified
source of extra tricks. Here Rubin's advance was well justified; he
must have been surprised to find partner with only five hearts. We
make it:

Pass–1,   6NT–1,   7♢–5,   7♡–4,   7NT–3

24. Too Much of a Good Thing

In the Round Robin of the 1979 Bermuda Bowl USA met Brazil on Vu-Graph. Eddie Kantar picked up this promising hand, sitting South at Game All:

♠ K 7
♡ A K J 9 5 4 3
♢ 3
♣ K Q 3

A two-heart opening would have been weak, so he opened one heart. The bidding unfolded in this way:

SOUTH	WEST	NORTH	EAST
1♡	Pass	2♣	Pass
3♡	Pass	5♡	Pass
?			

What do you make of partner's raise to five hearts? Is he enquiring specifically about the strength of your hearts, or is the bid just a natural slam try? Certainly it is strange that partner has found this jump when you hold two key honours in the suit that he bid first.

If you decide that your hand does merit a further effort, you could perhaps suggest a club slam instead of a heart slam. Indeed, holding both the top hearts and two honours in partner's suit, you may think you are entitled to advance to a grand slam.

These are the options:

(1) Pass   (2) 6♣   (3) 6♡   (4) 7♣   (5) 7♡

Game All   ♠ A Q J 8
Dealer South   ♡ 8
                    ◇ A K J 4
                    ♣ J 10 9 4

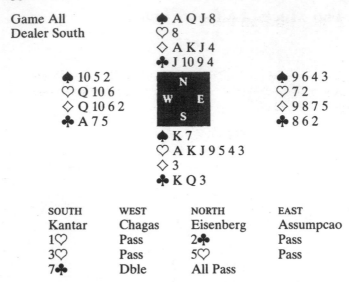

  ♠ 10 5 2   ♠ 9 6 4 3
  ♡ Q 10 6   ♡ 7 2
  ◇ Q 10 6 2   ◇ 9 8 7 5
  ♣ A 7 5   ♣ 8 6 2

                     ♠ K 7
                     ♡ A K J 9 5 4 3
                     ◇ 3
                     ♣ K Q 3

SOUTH	WEST	NORTH	EAST
Kantar	Chagas	Eisenberg	Assumpcao
1♡	Pass	2♣	Pass
3♡	Pass	5♡	Pass
7♣	Dble	All Pass	

Kantar decided he had enough for a grand. In case his partner
held two small hearts, along with six clubs to the ace and the
other two aces, he offered partner a choice of trump suit by
bidding 7♣. Chagas did not regard it as impolite to double and
the contract duly went one down.

Perhaps it was unfair of us to present you with the problem
Kantar faced, since his partner's initial 2♣ response was largely to
blame for the disaster. It was poor tactics to introduce a jack-high
suit on such a strong hand. Curiously, though, six hearts goes one
down and six clubs would have made.

Although we have some sympathy for Kantar's leap, there is
much to be said for caution when you are not absolutely sure of
the message partner is trying to pass. Having admitted that it was
an unfair problem, we make it:

       Pass–0,   6♣–5,   6♡–3,   7♣–3,   7♡–2

At the other table the Brazilian North, Branco, arrived in 6NT.
He won the spade lead, cashed ♡A, and led ♣K. Soloway took
his ace immediately and fired a diamond through, putting declarer
to a decision before he knew if the heart queen would drop.
Branco coolly inserted ◇J and a big swing went to Brazil.

25. Flat as a Pancake

Four teams contested the final stages of the British trials for the 1984 European Championships. On one critical board Raymond Brock sat North and picked up these cards:

♠ 8 6
♡ A 10 8 5 4
♢ A 7
♣ A J 9 8

With opponents vulnerable he opened one heart in the second seat and heard this continuation:

SOUTH	WEST	NORTH	EAST
–	Pass	1♡	Pass
3♣	Pass	4♣	Pass
4♡	Pass	?	

Only 13 points, yes, but you hold three aces and a good fit for the suit of partner's jump shift. If you do decide to investigate a slam, what is the best forward move? Should you bid Blackwood, cue-bid the control in diamonds, or simply blast into one or other slam?

If you are someone who acts best under pressure, we might add that the man across the table is Tony Forrester – a player who could be relied upon to draw the right inferences, and to expect his partner to do the same. These are the possibilities:

(1) Pass   (2) 4NT   (3) 5♢   (4) 6♣   (5) 6♡

East–West game   ♠ 8 6
Dealer West   ♡ A 10 8 5 4
                   ◇ A 7
                   ♣ A J 9 8

♠ K 10 5 4   ♠ J 9 3 2
♡ K 6 3 2   N   ♡ –
◇ K 10 9 6   W   E   ◇ Q J 8 5 4 2
♣ 2   S   ♣ 10 6 3

               ♠ A Q 7
               ♡ Q J 9 7
               ◇ 3
               ♣ K Q 7 5 4

SOUTH	WEST	NORTH	EAST
Forrester	Flint	Brock	Sheehan
–	Pass	1♡	Pass
3♣	Pass	4♣	Pass
4♡	Pass	6♣	All Pass

Flint made the bright start of a low heart, Forrester playing low from dummy. When Sheehan ruffed and returned a spade, declarer had to finesse and this led to two down. Six hearts would have been undefeatable.

Was North's decision to play in clubs unlucky or poorly judged? There are various reasons why it may be better to play in clubs. North's hearts are poor and if South holds such as ♡ K x x a 4–1 heart break may kill six hearts where six clubs would succeed. Also, a club slam will be played by South, with his spade holding (perhaps K x) protected from the opening lead. A final argument is that six clubs need not be the final word on the matter: South will have a chance to revert to six hearts.

Since North was always going to six, never to seven, there is little merit in Blackwood or a cue-bid. We make it:

     Pass–1,   4NT–2,   5◇–2,   6♣–5,   6♡–4

At the other table West opened 2♡, showing 11–15 points (!) and a 4–4–4–1 hand including hearts. East's two-spade response bought the contract and he managed to scramble eight tricks. With a grand slam in hearts possible the other way, he must have been disappointed to find it was a flat board (110 against 100).

26. All at Sea

From time to time cruise lines organise special holidays for bridge players. In the 1980s four famous players took part in a series televised on the Canberra liner. The best remembered deal was one where South held:

♠ A Q 9 7
♡ A K Q 5 4 2
◇ Q
♣ A K

With the opponents vulnerable, France's Christian Mari opened two clubs on these cards. The bidding continued:

SOUTH	WEST	NORTH	EAST
2♣	Pass	2◇	Pass
2♡	Pass	3♡	Pass
3♠	Pass	4◇	Pass
4NT	Pass	5♣	Pass
?			

Four diamonds was a cue-bid, with hearts agreed, but the subsequent no-ace response to Blackwood must mean that the cue-bid was made on the king. The choices at this point are to sign off in five hearts, to bid six hearts, or to use the only intermediate bid available – five diamonds. Which is your choice?

(1) 5◇   (2) 5♡   (3) 6♡

East–West game
Dealer South

```
                      ♠ 5 2
                      ♡ J 10 7
                      ◇ K
                      ♣ J 10 9 8 5 3 2
  ♠ 10 8 6 4                              ♠ K J 3
  ♡ 9 3             ┌─────────┐           ♡ 8 6
  ◇ A 9 5 3         │    N    │           ◇ J 10 8 7 6 4 2
  ♣ Q 6 4          W│         │E          ♣ 7
                    │    S    │
                    └─────────┘
                      ♠ A Q 9 7
                      ♡ A K Q 5 4 2
                      ◇ Q
                      ♣ A K
```

SOUTH	WEST	NORTH	EAST
Mari	Hamman	Mahmood	Forrester
2♣	Pass	2◇	Pass
2♡	Pass	3♡	Pass
3♠	Pass	4◇	Pass
4NT	Pass	5♣	Pass
6♡	All Pass		

Mari's jump to six hearts hardly seems justified. There is a sure
diamond loser and partner's ◇K won't help much; the slam is
likely to be at best on the spade finesse.

What of the alternatives? To sign off in 5♡, after Blackwood,
would lead to a missed slam when North held the vital ♠K.
Having taken the Blackwood route, South can consult his partner
further only with the intermediate bid of 5◇. That must mean, 'a
slam is still possible, but I need something extra from you.' We
make it:

$$5◇–5, \qquad 5♡–3, \qquad 6♡–1$$

Hamman led ♠4, South cashing two rounds, ruffing a third
round, and returning to his hand with a trump. When the fourth
round of spades was ruffed, East was able to discard his singleton
club. Mari played a diamond to West's ace and a club ruff by East
now put the contract one down.

Mari may have been feeling slightly sea-sick: if he employs the
'dangerous' entry, the club, before using the trump entry, he
makes the slam.

27. One for the Road

In 1990 sixteen world-class pairs, at La Haye in France, contested
an event known as the 'Cap Gemini Pandata'. The winners were
Eisenberg and Garozzo, closely followed by Forrester–Robson
and Meckstroth–Rodwell.

Brazil's Chagas and Branco, world champions at the time, had
a somewhat unimpressive auction on one board. North–South
were vulnerable and Chagas, South, held:

♠ A 3 2
♡ A K Q J 9 5 3
♢ –
♣ A 6 4

The bidding began:

SOUTH	WEST	NORTH	EAST
Chagas	Chemla	Branco	Mari
2♣	Pass	2♢	Pass
2♡	Pass	2♠	Pass
3♡	Pass	4NT	Pass
5♣	Pass	5NT	Pass
?			

North's 4NT was straightforward Blackwood, confirming hearts
as trumps, and South's response showed three (or zero) aces. The
subsequent 5NT bid suggested a grand slam.

What now? If you think you have already done enough you can
sign off, either in six hearts or six spades. If you think that your
solid hearts added to partner's spade suit will be enough for
thirteen tricks you can bid a direct seven hearts. A further
possibility is to mark time with six clubs, leaving it to partner to
decide on the final level. These are the possibilities:

(1) 6♣   (2) 6♡   (3) 6♠   (4) 7♡

Game all

Dealer South

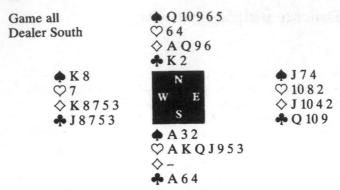

♠ Q 10 9 6 5
♡ 6 4
◇ A Q 9 6
♣ K 2

♠ K 8
♡ 7
◇ K 8 7 5 3
♣ J 8 7 5 3

♠ J 7 4
♡ 10 8 2
◇ J 10 4 2
♣ Q 10 9

♠ A 3 2
♡ A K Q J 9 5 3
◇ –
♣ A 6 4

Over Branco's 5NT Chagas (South) leapt to a grand slam in hearts – a considerable overbid, as we see it. He had already indicated his solid hearts and two outside aces. North was known to hold ◇A and if he held such as ♠ K Q J x x alongside he would (a) have responded two spades at his first turn, or (b) have bid the grand already. We mark it:

6♣–2,   6♡–5,   6♠–1,   7♡–2

The excitement was by no means over. Chagas won the club lead, ruffed a club, and ran his trumps to reach this ending:

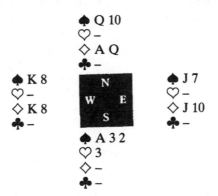

♠ Q 10
♡ –
◇ A Q
♣ –

♠ K 8
♡ –
◇ K 8
♣ –

♠ J 7
♡ –
◇ J 10
♣ –

♠ A 3 2
♡ 3
◇ –
♣ –

On the last trump Chemla parted with a spade! Chagas threw a diamond from dummy and scored the last three tricks.

28. Delicate Bid, Delicate Play

Sometimes you have to choose between four or five bids, none of which fits your hand exactly. That was the position on this board from the final of the Knockout Teams in the 1993 Bermuda Regional. The North players, first to speak at Love All, held these cards:

♠ A K 4
♡ K Q 7
♢ K 9 8 7 6 3
♣ 3

This was the start to the auction:

SOUTH	WEST	NORTH	EAST
–	–	1♢	Pass
1♡	Pass	?	

There are two separate problems now: should you rebid the diamonds or support the hearts? And should you rebid at the two level or the three level? A further possibility is an 'invented' rebid of one spade, waiting to hear more from across the table.

No other bids occur to us, so this is the list:

(1) 1♠   (2) 2♢   (3) 2♡   (4) 3♢   (5) 3♡

Love all   ♠ A K 4
Dealer North   ♡ K Q 7
                 ◇ K 9 8 7 6 3
                 ♣ 3

♠ Q 10 3 2   ♠ 8 5
♡ 9 5   N   ♡ 10 8 3 2
◇ J 10 4   W   E   ◇ Q 5
♣ Q J 9 8   S   ♣ K 10 7 6 5

                 ♠ J 9 7 6
                 ♡ A J 6 4
                 ◇ A 2
                 ♣ A 4 2

SOUTH	WEST	NORTH	EAST
–	–	1◇	Pass
1♡	Pass	3♡	Pass
4♣	Pass	4♠	Pass
4NT	Pass	5♠	Pass
6♡	All Pass		

The problem with three hearts is that it is not so convenient to
ruff with a trump holding of K Q x as it would be with, say, A x x.
Two diamonds and two hearts are both unenterprising and three
diamonds unattractive on such a moderate suit. It may not be
perfect but we incline rather to one spade, which leaves space to
find the best spot. We mark it:

     1♠–5,   2◇–2,   2♡–3,   3◇–2,   3♡–3

Here partner holds four spades, but this need not cause a
problem. A possible auction to the easy-to-make diamond slam
would be: 1◇–1♡, 1♠–2♣, 3♡–3♠, 4◇–6◇.

At the table a club was led against six hearts. South won with
the ace and played three rounds of diamonds, throwing a club.
The club return forced dummy to ruff, leaving the trump suit
blocked. Declarer now had to overtake a trump honour, going
one down when the suit broke 4–2. The opponents stopped in
game, eventually winning the event by just 6 IMPs.

In six hearts declarer should duck the first diamond, not the
third. Then, after the club ruff, he can use ◇A as an entry to
resolve the blockage in the trump suit.

29. Only Fair to Add

There is only one top bridge player known to the world at large: film star, Omar Sharif. For the 1995 Macallan International Pairs he formed a partnership with the most charismatic figure in the game, Zia Mahmood. Though not a practised partnership, they achieved a fine result in a pairs event of top international quality. On one deal Zia, sitting North at Game All, held:

♠ J 6 5
♡ A K 5
♢ A 10 9 7 2
♣ A K

After two passes he opened 2NT – certainly the best call on his hand. The bidding continued:

SOUTH	WEST	NORTH	EAST
Pass	Pass	2NT	Pass
3♢ (1)	Dble (2)	?	

(1) A transfer bid, indicating hearts.
(2) Strong diamonds, suggesting a diamond lead.

North has several possible calls. He has good support for partner's hearts and can bid hearts at the three level or, if he judges his support to be exceptional, at the four level. He might also bid game in no-trumps. A fourth possibility is to pass, leaving the next move to partner. Finally, North might redouble to show values in the 'transfer' suit – diamonds. These are the options:

(1) Pass   (2) Redouble   (3) 3♡   (4) 3NT   (5) 4♡

Game all
Dealer South

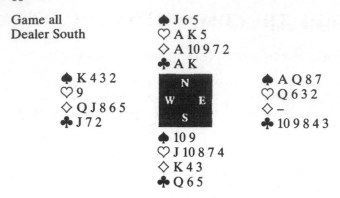

♠ J 6 5
♡ A K 5
◇ A 10 9 7 2
♣ A K

♠ K 4 3 2
♡ 9
◇ Q J 8 6 5
♣ J 7 2

♠ A Q 8 7
♡ Q 6 3 2
◇ –
♣ 10 9 8 4 3

♠ 10 9
♡ J 10 8 7 4
◇ K 4 3
♣ Q 6 5

SOUTH	WEST	NORTH	EAST
Sharif	Meckstroth	Mahmood	Rodwell
Pass	Pass	2NT	Pass
3◇	Dble	Rdble	All Pass

Zia's redouble was not dangerous since partner could retreat to
three hearts if he had a bad hand with one or two low diamonds.
What of the alternatives? Pass would be a bit weak, but three
hearts could not be criticised. As for 3NT, even if partner holds
♡ Q J x x x you will have only eight tricks; should he hold
anything more than that he will bid game himself. Four hearts is
an overbid, too. We make it:

    Pass–1,   Redouble–5,   3♡–3,   3NT–2,   4♡–1

A heart lead would probably beat three diamonds but
Meckstroth started with a low club. Preparing for a spade ruff,
Omar now led a spade. The defenders cashed two spade winners,
West switching to his singleton heart. Declarer won with the ace,
ruffed a spade, and led a second heart, on which West discarded a
club. Omar won with dummy's ♡K, cashed a second club and
crossed to ◇K. He now led ♣Q, ruffed and overruffed.

Omar had seven tricks by now, and with ◇ A 10 9 still in the
dummy it wasn't difficult to make two more. The famous
American pair, Meckstroth and Rodwell, didn't shine on this
deal, but it is only fair to add that they won the tournament by a
big margin.

PART III THE COMPETITIVE AUCTION

More points are won and lost during competitive auctions than in any other part of the game. In this section of the book you will have the chance to compare your judgement with that of the world's best players. Fear not! On several of the deals we have chosen, you will have every chance to outscore the experts. They don't always find the right bid, as you will see.

30. His Watch was Wrong

What match, in the history of the game, do you suppose attracted the greatest publicity? There's no doubt at all, it was the Battle of the Century, played in 1931–32 between Culbertson and Lenz. The day-by-day scores were front-page news in thirty different countries.

Culbertson had the amiable habit of arriving upwards of an hour late for most of the sessions. On an occasion when he was punctual he explained that his watch was wrong.

Critics at the time missed some of the attractions of a deal where Jacoby, South, held these cards at Love All:

$$\spadesuit\ J$$
$$\heartsuit\ K\ 9\ 3$$
$$\diamondsuit\ A\ K\ 5\ 2$$
$$\clubsuit\ A\ Q\ 9\ 4\ 2$$

The bidding began:

SOUTH	WEST	NORTH	EAST
–	–	–	Pass
1♣	Pass	3♣	3♠
?			

North's 3♣, in those days, was forcing. South now has a wide choice of calls. None of these would be wrong:

(1) Pass (2) 4♦ (3) 4♠ (4) 4NT (5) 5♣ (6) 6♣

Love all
Dealer East

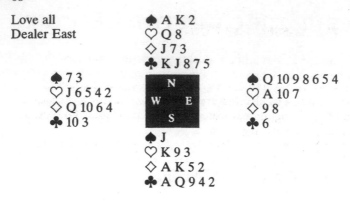

♠ A K 2
♡ Q 8
◇ J 7 3
♣ K J 8 7 5

♠ 7 3
♡ J 6 5 4 2
◇ Q 10 6 4
♣ 10 3

♠ Q 10 9 8 6 5 4
♡ A 10 7
◇ 9 8
♣ 6

♠ J
♡ K 9 3
◇ A K 5 2
♣ A Q 9 4 2

SOUTH	WEST	NORTH	EAST
Jacoby	Culbertson	Lenz	Mrs Culbertson
–	–	–	Pass
1♣	Pass	3♣	3♠
4♠	Pass	5♣	Pass
6♣	All Pass		

Although we offered 4NT in our list, such control-asking bids
were not then in vogue. The best natural bid available to Jacoby
was surely four diamonds, which might cause North to take an
unfavourable view of his J x x in the suit.

Jacoby said afterwards that he arbitrarily decided to contract
for a slam and bid four spades in the hope of averting a spade lead
(though what he would do with his singleton spade is not clear.)
Nowadays a Blackwood 4NT would be a fair alternative to four
diamonds. We make it:

Pass–1,   4◇–5,   4♠–2,   4NT–3,   5♣–1,   6♣–2

Mrs Culbertson had the misfortune to lead ♡A out of turn.
Jacoby then requested West to lead a diamond, as he was entitled
to in those days. When the jack held the play was over.

Jacoby remarked that a spade or club lead would have beaten
the slam, but that's not quite right. Declarer draws trumps, then
leads a low heart from the table. After the king has won he
throws a heart on the second spade, ruffs a spade, cashes ◇ A K,
and exits with a heart, leaving East on play.

31.   He Missed the Point

Would it surprise you to know that in the enlightened days of
1936 bridge was a weekly feature on the one television channel in
England? The programmes were presented by Hubert Phillips, a
famous journalist and a great wag.

A leading player of that time, Harry Ingram, included in his
'reminiscensies' (a word he could never spell) a deal where
Norman Bach sat North and held:

♠ Q 9 8 7 3 2
♡ 4
♢ –
♣ A K J 10 9 6

The player to his left (Ingram) opened with a vulnerable three
spades. Bach's partner, Kenneth Konstam, doubled this for
penalties. Two passes followed, then Ingram redoubled. Pass
from Konstam and four clubs from West. Norman Bach ventured
a double but then the auction took a strange turn:

SOUTH	WEST	NORTH	EAST
Kenneth	Kathleen	Norman	Harry
Konstam	Salmons	Bach	Ingram
–	–	–	3♠
Dble	Pass	Pass	Rdble
Pass	4♣	Dble	4♢
4♡	5♢	?	

Have you any idea what is going on? Possibilities that might
occur to you now are:

(1) Pass   (2) Double   (3) 5♠   (4) 6♣   (5) 6♠

Which of these would you favour, bearing in mind that you
have a fairly large audience?

Game all   ♠ Q 9 8 7 3 2
Dealer East   ♡ 4
                 ◇ –
                 ♣ A K J 10 9 6

♠ 4
♡ –
◇ K 9 8 7 2
♣ Q 8 7 5 4 3 2

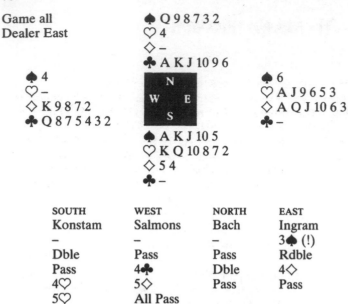

♠ 6
♡ A J 9 6 5 3
◇ A Q J 10 6 3
♣ –

♠ A K J 10 5
♡ K Q 10 8 7 2
◇ 5 4
♣ –

SOUTH	WEST	NORTH	EAST
Konstam	Salmons	Bach	Ingram
–	–	–	3♠ (!)
Dble	Pass	Pass	Rdble
Pass	4♣	Dble	4◇
4♡	5◇	Pass	Pass
5♡	All Pass		

Hubert's comment on the psychic 3♠ opening was that it made a nonsense of his painstakingly prepared commentary on how the bidding might go. The wily Ingram must have guessed that on a deal specially chosen for the programme his opponents would have a big spade fit.

Kenneth Konstam bid his hand reasonably. He had shown values in spades with his penalty double and felt entitled to mention his hearts subsequently (although East's antics might be thought to indicate a red two-suiter). Poor Norman Bach seems to have missed the point that East's redouble for rescue made no sense at all unless the opening bid was psychic. After South's strong bidding we think North is well worth 6♠ and mark it:

Pass–0,   Double–0,   5♠–2,   6♣–1,   6♠–5

As you may have surmised, five hearts did not play very well. It may have been the only time in history when a pair has gone five down in a 6–1 fit when there was a cold slam available in a 6–5 fit. Good entertainment for the viewers, at any rate!

32. Modest Recollection

A few decades ago the scoring method in European Championships was 2 points for a win (by 5 IMPs or more) and 1 for a tie. It made no different whether you won by 5 IMPs or 100 IMPs. The scheme used nowadays, where large numbers of VPs are at stake in every match, is better really. The players can never afford to relax; every board may be worth a victory point.

In the 1957 match between Britain and Ireland there was a board where South, with the opponents vulnerable, held these cards:

♠ 7 6 2
♡ A 10 8
♢ A 10 8 5 3
♣ 10 6

The auction started like this:

SOUTH	WEST	NORTH	EAST
–	–	–	Pass
Pass	1♡	Dble	Pass
2♢	2♡	3♢	3♡
?			

Partner will have a fair hand, although he may have intended to pass two diamonds had West not bid again. You yourself have values to spare for your original response and must now judge how strongly to compete. Which of these actions appeals to you?

(1) Double   (2) 3NT   (3) 4♢   (4) 5♢

East–West game   ♠ K 10 4
Dealer East   ♡ 2
                  ◇ K J 6 2
                  ♣ A Q 7 5 4

♠ A Q J   ♠ 9 8 5 3
♡ K Q J 7 4 3   **N**   ♡ 9 6 5
◇ 7 4   **W**   **E**   ◇ Q 9
♣ 9 2   **S**   ♣ K J 8 3

                  ♠ 7 6 2
                  ♡ A 10 8
                  ◇ A 10 8 5 3
                  ♣ 10 6

SOUTH	WEST	NORTH	EAST
Reese	O'Connell	Schapiro	O'Connell
–	–	–	Pass
Pass	1♡	Dble	Pass
2◇	2♡	3◇	3♡
5◇	All Pass		

Partner was unlikely to contribute towards a second heart stop, particularly after East's raise, so game in no-trumps was not attractive. Since North had advanced to the three level facing a partner who might hold very little, South's actual hand was likely to offer some play for eleven tricks in diamonds. We (still!) think that South's original choice looks best and mark it:

Double–2,   3NT–1,   4◇–2,   5◇–5

Barry, the Westerly of the O'Connell brothers, led the king of hearts. Declarer drew trumps and was able to establish a long club to discard one of his spade losers. That was 11 IMPs to Britain when Ireland went two down in 3NT at the other table.

A spade lead would have defeated five diamonds. North, who had bid strongly, was a big favourite to hold the king of spades. Since one or other opponent would surely hold a singleton heart, it was perhaps not impossible for West to find the spade lead – maybe even the queen, since with K x x x in dummy declarer might fail to cover.

33. Curtsey to the Queen

In 1957 a British Bridge World Par Contest was played in several countries, the deals composed by Terence Reese and Harold Franklin. On one hand North, fourth to speak at Love All, held:

♠ A 4 3 2
♡ A 10 7 5 4 3
♢ A 7 3
♣ –

This was the start to the suggested auction:

SOUTH	WEST	NORTH	EAST
–	–	–	1♢
4♠	Pass	?	

Various moves towards a slam are possible. You could try Blackwood, cue-bid the opponents' suit, make a grand-slam force of 5NT, or simply bid a direct six or seven spades. Bids in a new suit, five clubs or five hearts, are perhaps risky; some partners would take them as a cue-bid, others as natural. Let's restrict the list to these bids:

(1) 4NT   (2) 5♢   (3) 5NT   (4) 6♠   (5) 7♠

Love all   ♠ A 4 3 2
Dealer East   ♡ A 10 7 5 4 3
                    ◇ A 7 3
                    ♣ –

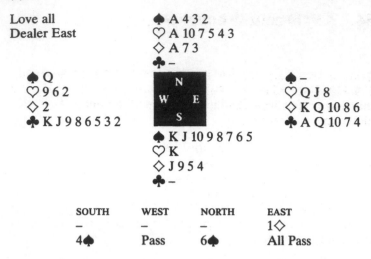

♠ Q   ♠ –
♡ 9 6 2   ♡ Q J 8
◇ 2   ◇ K Q 10 8 6
♣ K J 9 8 6 5 3 2   ♣ A Q 10 7 4

                    ♠ K J 10 9 8 7 6 5
                    ♡ K
                    ◇ J 9 5 4
                    ♣ –

SOUTH	WEST	NORTH	EAST
–	–	–	1◇
4♠	Pass	6♠	All Pass

If the spade suit contained more potential entries, such as
A 10 8 5, prospects of establishing the hearts would be better; it
would be natural to consider a grand slam. After a diamond lead,
however, the entry situation will not be strong. It may be –
probably will be – difficult to establish and run the hearts, even if
partner has a singleton. At the same time you certainly cannot
stop short of six. We mark it as follows:

     4NT–0,   5◇–3,   5NT–2,   6♠–5,   7♠–1

If your choice was five diamonds you might say 'I was going to
six spades anyway, so what's wrong with five diamonds on the
way?' The answer is that there is virtually no chance that partner
will do more than bid five spades; meanwhile the opponents will
have more chance to find a club sacrifice.

What of the play in six spades after the ◇2 lead? There is a
chance for a brilliancy, which in 1957 was found by three players –
Besse (Switzerland), Bourchtoff (France), and Blicher
(Denmark). After winning the diamond lead, cross to the king of
hearts and play a spade – letting West's queen hold!! Whatever
West plays now, you can easily bring in the hearts.

If we had wanted to make this hand difficult, remarked TR and
HF, we would have given West the singleton 6 of spades!

34. On Second Thoughts

Two powerful teams reached the final of the 1969 USA Spingold.
Bob Hamman and Bobby Wolff were on one side, although not at
that time partnering each other. At Love All Hamman, East,
picked up these cards:

♠ 8 7 6 4 3
♡ K 7
♢ A Q 9 6 5
♣ 6

His left-hand opponent opened with a weak two in spades and
the bidding continued:

SOUTH	WEST	NORTH	EAST
2♠	3♡	4♠	?

What's it to be? You can pass if you think it is the opponents'
hand. With five trumps, albeit small ones, a penalty double might
work well. Should you wish to contest you can bid five hearts, or
perhaps five diamonds – to show where your outside strength lies.
These are the main choices:

(1) Pass   (2) Double   (3) 5♢   (4) 5♡

Love all
Dealer South

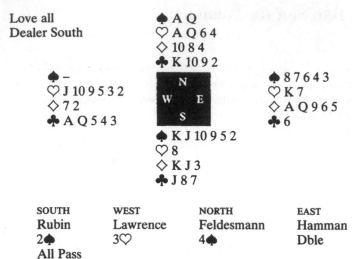

♠ A Q
♡ A Q 6 4
◇ 10 8 4
♣ K 10 9 2

♠ −
♡ J 10 9 5 3 2
◇ 7 2
♣ A Q 5 4 3

♠ 8 7 6 4 3
♡ K 7
◇ A Q 9 6 5
♣ 6

♠ K J 10 9 5 2
♡ 8
◇ K J 3
♣ J 8 7

SOUTH	WEST	NORTH	EAST
Rubin	Lawrence	Feldesmann	Hamman
2♠	3♡	4♠	Dble
All Pass			

It is tempting for East to double but, as you will see, his five trumps played a very small role. West led ♡J and, in view of his 3♡ overcall, you might expect declarer to finesse the queen. East would win and a club ruff would then beat the contract. No, Rubin called ♡A. He had taken the trouble to enquire about the opponents' style of leads. The jack denied a higher honour (the 10 would have been led from K J 10). Declarer drew trumps and ended with an overtrick.

Was Hamman unlucky to find his partner with so few points? The key to the hand is that North has bid four spades *despite being short in spades*. He is therefore bidding four spades to make and will hold considerably more points than your partner. With only two hearts, bidding on looks a poor idea. We make it:

Pass–5,   Double–2,   5◇–1,   5♡–1

At the other table Sam Stayman, West, passed over the 2♠ opening. North raised to 4♠ and Sam now contested with 4NT. He ended in five hearts doubled, which would have cost 900 (old scoring-table) on a trump lead. North led ♠A, though, and declarer scored two club ruffs to escape for 500.

35.   Battle of the Giants

There is a long-standing tradition that the team to represent USA in the Bermuda Bowl should win the right at the table, rather than be selected by some committee. (The same principle applies to their athletics team for the Olympics – reputations count for nothing and one race decides the matter.)

In 1970 four teams did battle to decide who would play in the 1971 Bermuda Bowl. On one board Altman, with the opponents vulnerable, picked up these West cards:

> ♠ 2
> ♡ A K 5
> ◇ A K 8 3 2
> ♣ K J 3 2

No doubt he was surprised to hear the player to his right open with a strong two clubs. He passed for the moment, then after two diamonds – pass – two spades, entered with a take-out double. The bidding continued like this:

SOUTH	WEST	NORTH	EAST
Grieve	Altman	Feldesmann	Stuart
–	–	–	Pass
2♣	Pass	2◇	Pass
2♠	Dble	Rdble	5♡
6♣	Dble	6♠	Pass
Pass	?		

Partner's five-heart bid is pre-emptive, obviously. You have a fair club holding sitting over declarer's second suit, not to mention your two ace–kings, and a penalty double must come into the reckoning. It's to be expected, though, that South will have a very distributional hand.

The other possibilities are to sacrifice in seven hearts or to pass. Which would be your choice?

(1) Pass   (2) Double   (3) 7♡

North–South game
Dealer East

```
                    ♠ J 10 8 4 3
                    ♡ 10 9 2
                    ◇ Q J 10 6
                    ♣ 7
   ♠ 2                               ♠ 7
   ♡ A K 5           N               ♡ Q J 7 6 4 3
   ◇ A K 8 3 2    W     E            ◇ 9 7 5 4
   ♣ K J 3 2         S               ♣ 9 8
                    ♠ A K Q 9 6 5
                    ♡ 8
                    ◇ –
                    ♣ A Q 10 6 5 4
```

SOUTH	WEST	NORTH	EAST
Grieve	Altman	Feldesmann	Stuart
–	–	–	Pass
2♣	Pass	2◇	Pass
2♠	Dble	Rdble	5♡
6♣	Dble	6♠	Pass
Pass	Dble	All Pass	

Altman elected to double six spades but the contract was easily
made. Many would do the same but some warning signs were
there. North's redouble had promised a spade fit and with so
many high cards missing South would scarcely have advanced to
the six level on less than a 6–6 distribution in the black suits.

West held four clubs himself and if the suit lay 4–1–2–6 round
the table, with dummy holding the singleton, it was entirely
possible that six spades might succeed.

What was the likely cost of a sacrifice in seven hearts? A fair
estimate would be about 500. It's hard to judge impartially when
you know the outcome of a hand. Call us result merchants but we
are going to award top marks to the seven-heart sacrifice.

Pass–2,   Double–2,   7♡–5

At the other table East opened 3♡! South doubled, for take-
out, and West raised to 4♡. When this ran back to South he bid
just 4♠. West doubled and South quickly racked up +1190. He
must have been disappointed to lose 10 IMPs on the board.

36. Upward Climb

Sometimes you hold a useful-looking hand for slam purposes, but
no aces. This was the situation on a deal from a Camrose match
between England and Scotland. Vulnerable against not, the
Scottish North held:

♠ K 2
♡ Q 8
♢ K 10 7 6 3
♣ K 10 9 6

He passed as dealer, the next player passed, and his partner
opened one diamond in third position. The bidding continued:

SOUTH	WEST	NORTH	EAST
–	–	Pass	Pass
1♢	1♡	3♢	3♡
4♡	Pass	?	

What would you say next? If you think you know enough
already, you may sign off in five diamonds or leap to six
diamonds. If you are uncertain, you could cue-bid four spades or
perhaps wheel out the old Black. These are the possibilities:

(1) 4♣   (2) 4NT   (3) 5♢   (4) 6♢

North–South game
Dealer North

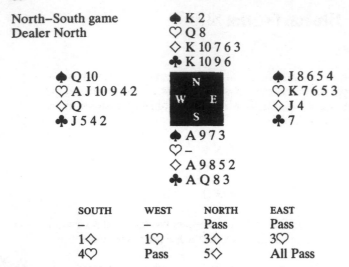

```
                    ♠ K 2
                    ♡ Q 8
                    ◇ K 10 7 6 3
                    ♣ K 10 9 6
  ♠ Q 10                              ♠ J 8 6 5 4
  ♡ A J 10 9 4 2        N             ♡ K 7 6 5 3
  ◇ Q              W         E        ◇ J 4
  ♣ J 5 4 2             S             ♣ 7
                    ♠ A 9 7 3
                    ♡ –
                    ◇ A 9 8 5 2
                    ♣ A Q 8 3
```

SOUTH	WEST	NORTH	EAST
–	–	Pass	Pass
1◇	1♡	3◇	3♡
4♡	Pass	5◇	All Pass

The Scottish North contended later that with no aces there
wasn't much else he could do after four hearts. That was very
feeble, of course. If his partner wanted to hear about aces he
would have bid 4NT rather than four hearts. North's three kings
would plug three gaps in partner's hand; South was odds-on to
hold a heart void and this all added up to excellent slam
prospects.

This is how we mark North's alternatives:

$$4♠–5, \quad 4NT–2, \quad 5◇–0, \quad 6◇–3$$

At the other table South jumped to five diamonds over East's
three hearts. This was not particularly helpful, and North passed.

Even seven diamonds is a very fair contract. Declarer will, of
course, test the distribution in spades and diamonds to decide
which opponent, if either, may hold length in clubs.

On these hands from a by-gone era it is interesting to
contemplate how the bidding would go today. Most West players
would make a weak jump overcall of two hearts, rather than one
heart, after which North would not be able to show his values so
easily. Some partnerships would be able to open on the East cards
– perhaps with 2NT, showing a weak hand with the majors or the
minors. Not so easy for North–South then!

37.   Reach for the Sky

One of the biggest swings in the 1976 world championship occurred in the round-robin clash between Australia and the mighty Italians. Longhurst sat North for the Aussies and picked up this hand:

♠ K 2
♡ A 7 3
◇ J 8 7
♣ Q J 9 7 6

First in hand at Game All, he passed. His partner, South, opened one club and the auction developed like this:

SOUTH	WEST	NORTH	EAST
–	–	Pass	Pass
1♣	1♡	2♡	4♡
4♠	5♡	?	

The cue-bid of two hearts showed initially a sound raise to (at least) three clubs. Partner has now shown a black two-suiter and you have some good cards for him. Do your values justify a bid of six clubs, do you think? If not, the choice is between pass and double.

The only clue we will give you . . . not much help, we agree . . . is that a large number of IMPs hang on your decision. These are the options:

(1) Pass   (2) Double   (3) 6♣

Game all   ♠ K 2
Dealer North   ♡ A 7 3
                   ◇ J 8 7
                   ♣ Q J 9 7 6

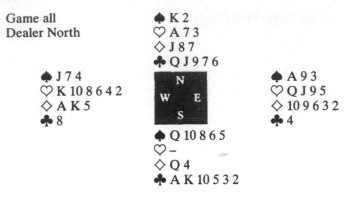

♠ J 7 4   ♠ A 9 3
♡ K 10 8 6 4 2   ♡ Q J 9 5
◇ A K 5   ◇ 10 9 6 3 2
♣ 8   ♣ 4

                   ♠ Q 10 8 6 5
                   ♡ –
                   ◇ Q 4
                   ♣ A K 10 5 3 2

SOUTH	WEST	NORTH	EAST
Klinger	Forquet	Longhurst	Belladonna
–	–	Pass	Pass
1♣	1♡	2♡	4♡
4♠	5♡	6♣	Pass
Pass	Dble	All Pass	

Longhurst had already shown most of his values and with the opponents bidding to the five level, vulnerable, there was a good chance that his ♡A faced a void. Had he held ◇A instead, six clubs would have had some play. We see it like this:

$$\text{Pass–3,}\quad\text{Double–5,}\quad\text{6♣–1}$$

If North had doubled five hearts and led ♠K his side would have collected 800. As it was, the Italians cashed two diamonds and a spade against six clubs doubled, scoring 500.

This was the auction in the other room:

SOUTH	WEST	NORTH	EAST
Garozzo	Seres	Franco	Smilde
–	–	Pass	Pass
1♠	2♡	Dble	4♡
5♣	Dble	All Pass	

East–West collected 200. North's miscalculation at the first table meant that Australia lost 7 IMPs instead of winning 14.

38.   Call my Bluff

In the final of the 1976 Bermuda Bowl there was a clash of the giants – Italy against North America. After 75 boards (out of 96) the Americans led by just 170–152. Belladonna, who was fourth to speak on the next board, picked up this splendid collection:

♠ 3
♡ 5
♢ A Q 7
♣ A K Q J 8 6 5 2

As sometimes happens when you hold a powerful hand in the fourth scat, the other three players all found something to say:

SOUTH	WEST	NORTH	EAST
–	2♠ (1)	Dble	4♠
?			

(1) Weak two, 6–10 points.

Both sides are vulnerable, so the opponents will have plenty of distribution for their bidding. You are missing three key cards, the diamond king and the major-suit aces. Is there any scientific way to discover how many of these partner holds? Or should you simply blast into some contract or other, perhaps putting the opponents under pressure to sacrifice?

These are the actions to be considered:

(1) 4NT   (2) 5♣   (3) 5♠   (4) 6♣   (5) 7♣

Game all   ♠ 8
Dealer West   ♡ A K 10 7 3
                  ♢ K J 10 9 2
                  ♣ 7 3

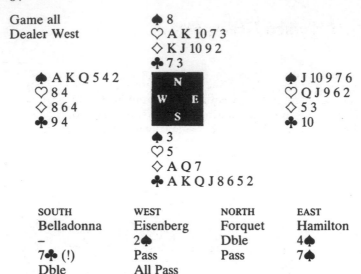

♠ A K Q 5 4 2   ♠ J 10 9 7 6
♡ 8 4   ♡ Q J 9 6 2
♢ 8 6 4   ♢ 5 3
♣ 9 4   ♣ 10

                  ♠ 3
                  ♡ 5
                  ♢ A Q 7
                  ♣ A K Q J 8 6 5 2

SOUTH	WEST	NORTH	EAST
Belladonna	Eisenberg	Forquet	Hamilton
–	2♠	Dble	4♠
7♣ (!)	Pass	Pass	7♠
Dble	All Pass		

Can you believe that in a world championship final the Italian
maestro would dare to leap to seven with a loser in the opponents'
suit? The American East, Hamilton, was unwilling to call
Belladonna's bluff and sacrificed in seven spades, going down
1400. This was the bidding at the other table:

SOUTH	WEST	NORTH	EAST
Paulsen	Garozzo	Ross	Franco
–	2♠	3♡	4♠
6♣	All Pass		

The spade ace was led and North–South collected 1370. So, the
reward for Belladonna's bravery (if that's the word that occurs to
you) was a mere 1 IMP. Of course, Giorgio had a bigger price in
mind – to make the grand on a non-spade lead.

To the marking. No benefit will come from a cue-bid of 5♠,
nor will Blackwood help much. Indeed, many would regard 4NT
as a request to choose a suit. We included 5♣ as a make-weight
and the normal bid on the hand would surely be 6♣. We'll mark
it:

    4NT–1,   5♣–0,   5♠–0,   6♣–5,   7♣–4

39. It Looked Great, But . . .

When you have opened light and been supported by your partner,
can it ever be right to follow with a penalty double on the next
round? The question arose during the qualifying round of the
1979 Bermuda Bowl. With neither side vulnerable South held:

♠ 8 7 3
♡ A J 9 7 2
◇ –
♣ A J 10 8 7

Most players would rate this as an opening bid and the
Australian South, playing against Italy, began with one heart. The
bidding continued:

SOUTH	WEST	NORTH	EAST
J. Borin	Pittala	N. Borin	Belladonna
1♡	Pass	3♡	4♠
?			

There are a number of possibilities now, the more so since
Belladonna is known to be a pretty venturesome bidder. How
would you mark these alternatives:

(1) Pass   (2) Double   (3) 5♣   (4) 5♡

A similar decision arose at the other table:

SOUTH	WEST	NORTH	EAST
Garozzo	Cummings	Lauria	Seres
1♡	Pass	4♡	4♠
?			

It should be mentioned that Lauria's raise to four hearts, as in
most modern systems, had a pre-emptive ring to it.

Love all
Dealer South

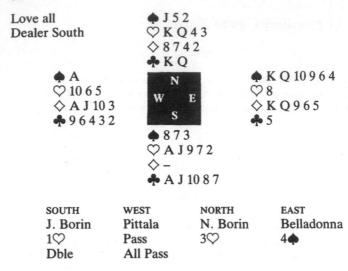

```
                    ♠ J 5 2
                    ♡ K Q 4 3
                    ◇ 8 7 4 2
                    ♣ K Q
♠ A                                    ♠ K Q 10 9 6 4
♡ 10 6 5              N                ♡ 8
◇ A J 10 3      W          E           ◇ K Q 9 6 5
♣ 9 6 4 3 2          S                 ♣ 5
                    ♠ 8 7 3
                    ♡ A J 9 7 2
                    ◇ –
                    ♣ A J 10 8 7
```

SOUTH	WEST	NORTH	EAST
J. Borin	Pittala	N. Borin	Belladonna
1♡	Pass	3♡	4♠
Dble	All Pass		

South has a difficult call over 4♠, there is no doubt of that. A double may lead to a small penalty, but are you going to risk underleading ♡A? In our view South's best choice is to pass, leaving the final move to partner. We make it:

Pass–5,   Double–2,   5♣–3,   5♡–2

Jim Borin chose to double, while at the other table Garozzo passed and North doubled four spades. Two underleads of an ace are required to beat four spades. Garozzo started well with a low heart but Lauria then played ♣K before switching to a diamond. +590 to the Australians. At the other table the defence was ace and another heart, Belladonna gaining 3 IMPs for his +690.

Only one pair beat four spades. For the Far East, Kuo led ♡9, a high heart (McKenney) requesting a diamond return. Huang won with the queen and returned ◇2, McKenney for clubs. Kuo ruffed and duly led a club to the queen to receive his second ruff. It looked great, but the Far Easterners lost 13 IMPs when Kantar–Eisenberg made five hearts doubled. (At double dummy South can make twelve tricks after a spade lead and – rather remarkably – thirteen tricks against any other lead.)

40.   Pressure Cooker

Great Britain met the USA in the final of the 1984 Women's
Olympiad. On an early board, first to speak at Game All, Sandra
Landy picked up these cards in the North seat:

♠ Q 8 7 3
♡ 10
◇ A Q 10 7 2
♣ K 8 3

Whether this is a sound opening bid, vulnerable, is a matter of
opinion. One possibility is to pass and hope later to be able to
make a take-out double of hearts. Never one to rest on the side
lines, Landy opened one diamond and the bidding developed as
follows:

SOUTH	WEST	NORTH	EAST
Horton	Sanders	Landy	Kennedy
–	–	1◇	1♡
1♣	2♠	?	

Your partner is likely to hold a 5-card spade suit (with a 4-card
suit she would start with a negative double). West's two spades
proclaimed a sound raise to at least three hearts. What would you
say now?

If you are somewhat ashamed of having opened on a moderate
11-count you may think a pass appropriate. To show that you
have support for the spades you might double the opponent's
spade cue-bid or raise spades to the three level. There may be
tactical value in a raise to four spades. That completes the list,
surely.

(1) Pass   (2) Double   (3) 3♠   (4) 4♠

Game all
Dealer North

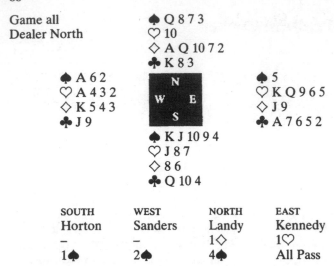

```
                    ♠ Q 8 7 3
                    ♡ 10
                    ◇ A Q 10 7 2
                    ♣ K 8 3
        ♠ A 6 2                        ♠ 5
        ♡ A 4 3 2                      ♡ K Q 9 6 5
        ◇ K 5 4 3                      ◇ J 9
        ♣ J 9                          ♣ A 7 6 5 2
                    ♠ K J 10 9 4
                    ♡ J 8 7
                    ◇ 8 6
                    ♣ Q 10 4
```

SOUTH	WEST	NORTH	EAST
Horton	Sanders	Landy	Kennedy
–	–	1◇	1♡
1♠	2♠	4♠	All Pass

The value bid on the North hand is three spades. It's easy to see what will happen next, though; the opponents will bid four hearts and you will have another decision to make. Sandra Landy found the pressure bid of four spades. The advantage of this is that the opponents have to make the final decision – not you!

A double of two spades would not help much, and in any case would suggest a hand with points rather than distributional support. You might pass over two spades, to see how high the opponents go under their own steam. We like Landy's effort best, however, and mark it:

Pass–1,   Double–0,   3♠–3,   4♠–5

Four hearts by East goes one down after a diamond lead, the third round of diamonds promoting a trump trick. Against Landy's four spades Sanders led ♡A and switched to ♣J. The defenders can now score a club ruff if East holds up the ace of clubs. Landy called for dummy's king, though, and East pounced with the ace. That was +620 for the Brits.

At the other table North passed and East–West had an uninterrupted auction to three hearts, played by West. Ten tricks could not be prevented, with North on lead, and the resultant 170 gave Britain a swing of 13 IMPs.

41. Final Straight

In the quarter-final of the 1984 Olympiad the USA, with four
boards to go, led Austria by 121–103. The Austrians then staged
an amazing rally, beginning on board 61, where at Game All
Bobby Wolff, sitting West, held:

♠ K
♡ A 7 5 3
♢ K Q 8 4 3
♣ A J 8

Terraneo, in front of him, dealt and opened one diamond, a
nebulous call in the one-club system he was playing.

SOUTH	WEST	NORTH	EAST
1♢	?	–	–

What strikes you as best now? When you are strong in the suit
opened, Pass is always a possibility. If that's not your style, then
you could enter with one heart, with 1NT, or – if you are willing
to turn a blind eye to the shortage in spades – with a double.
This is the list:

(1) Pass   (2) Double   (3) 1♡   (4) 1NT

Game all   ♠ Q 10 7 5 2   Board 61
Dealer South   ♡ 10 4 2
                   ◇ 7 6 5
                   ♣ 7 3

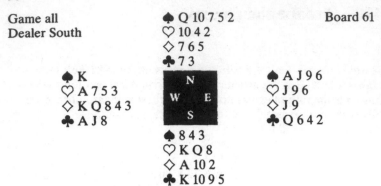

	♠ K	♠ A J 9 6
	♡ A 7 5 3	♡ J 9 6
	◇ K Q 8 4 3	◇ J 9
	♣ A J 8	♣ Q 6 4 2

                   ♠ 8 4 3
                   ♡ K Q 8
                   ◇ A 10 2
                   ♣ K 10 9 5

With 26 points between them, the Americans passed out
South's one diamond opening. The contract went four down – 400
to the USA. At the other table Austria made 3NT + 1, gaining 6
IMPs.

West has no very comfortable action over one diamond. We
make 1NT the best of a bad bunch and give these marks:

         Pass–2,   Double–2,   1♡–1,   1NT–5

The Austrians gained heavily on the next two boards as well,
giving them a 7-IMP lead with just this one board to play:

North–South game   ♠ J 4 3   Board 64
Dealer South   ♡ K 9 5
                   ◇ J 8
                   ♣ A Q J 9 8

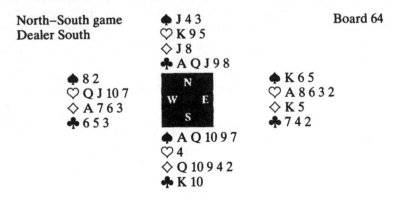

	♠ 8 2	♠ K 6 5
	♡ Q J 10 7	♡ A 8 6 3 2
	◇ A 7 6 3	◇ K 5
	♣ 6 5 3	♣ 7 4 2

                   ♠ A Q 10 9 7
                   ♡ 4
                   ◇ Q 10 9 4 2
                   ♣ K 10

Both teams made 4♠. But suppose the US East had overtaken
♡Q lead and switched to ◇K. One down and the Olympic title!

42.   One for the Courts

Austria met USA once again in the finals of the 1985 Bermuda
Bowl. It had been a long tournament and general opinion at the
time was that the play was not of the highest standard. There was
plenty of interest in this deal, where Fucik sat South for the
Austrians and held this hand:

♠ K 9 4 3
♡ A K Q J 7 6
♢ 8
♣ 10 5

With the opponents vulnerable, the bidding (at both tables, in
fact) started like this:

SOUTH	WEST	NORTH	EAST
–	–	Pass	1♠
2♡	Pass	3♢	Pass
?			

Considering that you made just a simple overcall on the
previous round, you have something in hand and may think three
hearts not enough now. You will not be surprised to find four
hearts in our list below. What about 3NT, though? Nine tricks
might be easier to find than ten. Against that, there is no
guarantee that partner will stop the clubs.

Some players like to bid the opponent's suit whenever they
have a strong hand and the going becomes difficult. That surely
completes our list.

(1) 3♡   (2) 3NT   (3) 3♠   (4) 4♡

East–West game ♠ J 10
Dealer North ♡ 10 3
♢ K Q J 10 7 3
♣ K 9 8

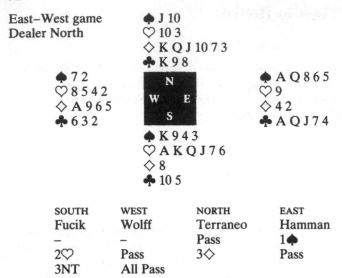

♠ 7 2
♡ 8 5 4 2
♢ A 9 6 5
♣ 6 3 2

♠ A Q 8 6 5
♡ 9
♢ 4 2
♣ A Q J 7 4

♠ K 9 4 3
♡ A K Q J 7 6
♢ 8
♣ 10 5

SOUTH	WEST	NORTH	EAST
Fucik	Wolff	Terraneo	Hamman
–	–	Pass	1♠
2♡	Pass	3♢	Pass
3NT	All Pass		

Partner was likely to provide enough bits and pieces to give 3NT a play and we like that call best. Three spades would surely request a spade stop, not show one. We mark it:

$$3\heartsuit{-}1, \quad 3NT{-}5, \quad 3\spadesuit{-}0, \quad 4\heartsuit{-}3$$

Defending 3NT, Hamman won the spade lead and returned a heart, a clever attack on declarer's communications. Fucik won with the ace and played a diamond. West rose correctly with the ace and, holding no club higher than the 8, played another spade. Hamman had to cover dummy's honour; declarer could now cash two spade tricks and cross to ♡10 to score five tricks in diamonds. +400.

At the other table Pender preferred to rebid 4♡ on the South cards. The defence began with a spade to the ace, a diamond to the ace, and a club switch. One down.

Or was it? The Americans protested that West's defence had been aided by the fact that the diamond switch had been made only after considerable thought (not the way they lead a singleton at the local church hall). The appeals committee agreed and the board was re-scored as 420 to North–South. East should have switched to a trump at trick 2, denying a singleton diamond.

43. Time to Retire

Nine-card suits don't grow on trees, and when you hold one in the fourth seat you don't expect to have the auction all to yourself. In a match between Canada and Portugal the South players, vulnerable against not, picked up:

♠ A K Q 8 7 5 4 3 2
♡ –
♢ J 9
♣ 5 4

West, on their left, opened one club. North passed and East responded one heart. Some players would try a semi-psychic one spade now, intending to bid four spades on the next round. Is that likely to deceive anyone? A better scheme, if you propose to be clever, is to bid three spades. It is unlikely that this will be passed out, and when on the next round you follow with four spades the opponents will not expect that you hold nine solid tricks.

One South player did follow such a scheme (we will see how he fared in a moment). The other bid a straightforward four spades on the first round and the bidding continued:

SOUTH	WEST	NORTH	EAST
–	1♣	Pass	1♡
4♠	5♡	Dble	Pass
?			

Should you accept partner's invitation to defend, do you think, or should you pull the double to some number of spades? The decision will depend largely on how much you expect partner to have for you in the minors? The alternatives are:

(1) Pass   (2) 5♠   (3) 6♠

North–South game
Dealer West

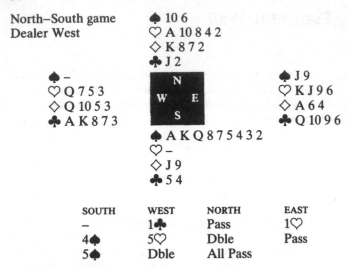

♠ 10 6
♡ A 10 8 4 2
♦ K 8 7 2
♣ J 2

♠ –
♡ Q 7 5 3
♦ Q 10 5 3
♣ A K 8 7 3

♠ J 9
♡ K J 9 6
♦ A 6 4
♣ Q 10 9 6

♠ A K Q 8 7 5 4 3 2
♡ –
♦ J 9
♣ 5 4

SOUTH	WEST	NORTH	EAST
–	1♣	Pass	1♡
4♠	5♡	Dble	Pass
5♠	Dble	All Pass	

This went one down. The opponents would probably have gone
two down, so South's five spades made a difference of 500 points.
Everyone except North was inclined to agree with South's five
spades. 'I would have gone to six on his hand,' was the comment
of one well-known journalist.

Let's look at the matter more closely from South's angle. Was it
not clear that North had doubled on the strength of a trick or two
in hearts? If instead he held top tricks in the minors he would
surely have preferred to raise the spades.

It was unlikely that North would cover two of South's four
minor-suit losers. So, although most players would advance –
perhaps unthinkingly – to five spades, it was not the correct move.
We mark it like this:

Pass–5,   5♠–2,   6♠–0

At the other table South started with a deceptive three spades,
going to four spades over West's raise to four hearts. East
doubled and West led ♣ A K, followed by a low diamond.
Declarer guessed correctly to play low and that was +790. A
possible defence was ace of clubs, club to the queen, and a switch
to ♠9. To make the contract then, declarer would have to run
this to dummy's 10!

44. Ear to the Wall

How do you react when the opponents bid unexpectedly high and you hold a good hand? On this deal, from the 1992 Australian Butler Trials, Ron Klinger had to bear in mind too that the opponents were vulnerable. Fourth to speak, he held these cards:

♠ A 6 3
♡ 2
♢ A Q J 10 8 7
♣ A K 7

With East–West vulnerable the auction begins:

SOUTH	WEST	NORTH	EAST
–	Pass	Pass	1♠
Dble	2NT (1)	Pass	4♠
?			

(1) Sound raise to three spades.

North–South hold at most 22 points between them, yet have soared to four spades in just three bids. You have four likely quick tricks against this contract and on that basis might well prefer a double to a pass. How about bidding on, though? It seems that partner will be short in spades and he may well hold some length in diamonds.

We have covered the only possibilities. What is your choice from:

(1) Pass   (2) Double   (3) 5♢ ?

East–West game
Dealer West

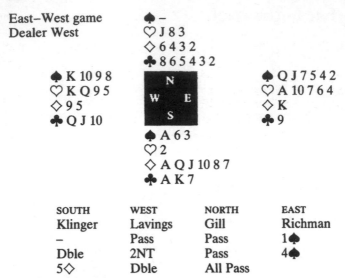

	♠ –	
	♡ J 8 3	
	◇ 6 4 3 2	
	♣ 8 6 5 4 3 2	

♠ K 10 9 8
♡ K Q 9 5
◇ 9 5
♣ Q J 10

♠ Q J 7 5 4 2
♡ A 10 7 6 4
◇ K
♣ 9

♠ A 6 3
♡ 2
◇ A Q J 10 8 7
♣ A K 7

SOUTH	WEST	NORTH	EAST
Klinger	Lavings	Gill	Richman
–	Pass	Pass	1♠
Dble	2NT	Pass	4♠
5◇	Dble	All Pass	

Since the opponents were vulnerable, Klinger could tell that
East would have a distributional hand to justify his game bid.
There was therefore no guarantee that two rounds of clubs would
stand up.

In any case, even if the spade game did go one down, it was
possible that five diamonds would be on. He duly bid the diamond
game, which West decided to double. The game proved an easy
make and North–South recorded +750. Since the datum (the
average North–South score on the board) was –220, this was
worth 14 IMPs.

We might perhaps have offered you West's hand, to see how
you would react to five diamonds. No doubt Lavings expected his
hearts to play a role in the defence but this was not certain after
South's sequence. Had West passed, it is at least possible that his
partner might have saved a few points by advancing to five
spades, going one down doubled.

Despite the fact that many Souths must have judged the hand
poorly when it arose, we don't find it a difficult problem to mark.
There were several indicators in favour of bidding five diamonds
and we make it:

Double–2,   Pass–1,   5◇–5

45. High Premium

The teams of Zia Mahmood and Eddie Kantar met in the 64-board final of the 1988 Spring Nationals. Zia held a small lead as the respective South players picked up:

♠ –
♡ K 7
♢ A 3 2
♣ K Q J 10 8 6 5 2

With the opponents vulnerable, they opened one club. The next player passed and the North players made a pre-emptive response in diamonds (two diamonds in one room, three diamonds in the other). East entered with four spades and the bidding continued like this at both tables:

SOUTH	WEST	NORTH	EAST
1♣	Pass	(2♢ or 3♢)	4♠
5♣	5♠	Pass	6♠
?			

Seven clubs will not cost much, so the task is to calculate the prospects of six spades. How many tricks is your hand worth in defence, do you think? Not for the first time, the options are to pass, to double, or to bid:

(1) Pass   (2) Double   (3) 7♣

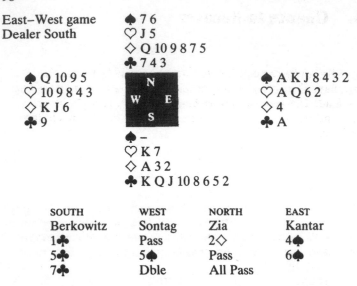

East–West game
Dealer South

♠ 7 6
♡ J 5
♢ Q 10 9 8 7 5
♣ 7 4 3

♠ Q 10 9 5
♡ 10 9 8 4 3
♢ K J 6
♣ 9

♠ A K J 8 4 3 2
♡ A Q 6 2
♢ 4
♣ A

♠ –
♡ K 7
♢ A 3 2
♣ K Q J 10 8 6 5 2

SOUTH	WEST	NORTH	EAST
Berkowitz	Sontag	Zia	Kantar
1♣	Pass	2♢	4♠
5♣	5♠	Pass	6♠
7♣	Dble	All Pass	

Berkowitz took out insurance in 7♣, as many would have done.
Still, it cost 500 and 6♠ would have failed, a net loss of 600. Let's
look at the mathematics of the situation. The premium for the
insurance, as we have seen, was 600. Had South passed, and
suffered the result he feared – six spades making, the pass would
cost him 1430 − 500, that's 930. So, at aggregate scoring you
should sacrifice unless you think the slam will fail more than 60%
of the time. It's closer at IMPs, more like 14 IMPs against 12.

What are the prospects of six spades? East is likely to hold ♡A,
so there's a fair chance that your ♡K will score. The ♢A *might*
be ruffed but in that case a club trick is possible. East cannot have
bid the slam with any certainty since his partner's 5♠ might have
had an element of sacrifice to it. We rate the chance of six spades
failing quite highly and give these marks:

Pass–5,   Double–2,   7♣–2

The other South, Mohan, also bid 7♣. This was more
attractive, facing a 3♢ response, since ♢A had lost some of its
glitter.

46. Chance to Recover

Great Britain met Austria in the final of the 1992 Women's Olympiad. The British team started strongly and soon opened up a big lead. The Austrians were back on terms, though, by the time Sandra Landy – at Love All – picked up these cards in the South seat:

♠ A Q
♡ Q 6 4
♢ 9 8 6 4 3
♣ A 10 8

Weigkricht, to her right, opened with a natural call of two clubs. Landy passed and the auction continued:

SOUTH	WEST	NORTH	EAST
Landy	Fischer	Handley	Weigkricht
–	–	–	2♣ (1)
Pass	2♠	Dble	3♣
?			

(1) Natural, 11–16 points.

Partner may be assumed to hold length in both red suits. If you think that your combined values will be enough for game, you can bid five diamonds or perhaps four hearts. Another possibility is that your ♣10 will pull some weight in 3NT. Partner might hold ♣ J x or a singleton jack.

If you view game prospects as uncertain you can bid an invitational four diamonds. The final possibility is a penalty double of three clubs. Plenty of options, then:

(1) Double   (2) 3NT   (3) 4♢   (4) 4♡   (5) 5♢

Love all   ♠ 10 7 6 4
Dealer East   ♡ A J 3 2
                  ♢ A K 10 7
                  ♣ 7

♠ K J 9 8 3 2   ♠ 5
♡ 8 7 5   ♡ K 10 9
♢ J 5   N   ♢ Q 2
♣ 5 4   W   E   ♣ K Q J 9 6 3 2
               S

                ♠ A Q
                ♡ Q 6 4
                ♢ 9 8 6 4 3
                ♣ A 10 8

SOUTH	WEST	NORTH	EAST
Landy	Fischer	Handley	Weigkricht
–	–	–	2♣
Pass	2♠	Dble	3♣
3NT	All Pass		

West had very little and a penalty double of 3♣ would have worked handsomely. At double-dummy the defenders can cash two diamonds and ♠A, then exit with ace and another trump. Declarer would have to open the hearts and would be three down.

Five diamonds is also an excellent spot, declarer making an overtrick by discarding a spade on the hearts. Landy, perhaps seduced by her ♣10, opted for 3NT. It's worth noting, though, that any contribution partner might make towards a second club stop would also assist in the defence to three clubs. We mark it:

Double–3,   3NT–2,   4♢–1,   4♡–2,   5♢–5

Fischer led a club against 3NT and Landy won immediately. The diamonds broke 2–2 and she proceeded to run the suit. The contract might now have been made. East had to retain a guard to her ♡K. Declarer could have cashed ♠A, drawing East's singleton in that suit, then end-played her with ♣10.

Landy didn't play to her usual form, taking a finesse in hearts and going one down. It was an expensive slip, since the Austrians misjudged the board in the other room, stopping in three diamonds. Austria went on to win the final by 48 IMPs.

47. Spiral Staircase

During the qualifying stages of the 1992 Olympiad Hong Kong met Brazil. With only the opponents vulnerable, Chun, East for Hong Kong, picked up this hand:

♠ J 10 5
♡ J
♢ K 7 5 4 2
♣ 9 7 6 2

The Brazilian to his left opened one spade and the next player, Chiu, entered with three diamonds, a conventional bid which indicated a red two-suiter. His right-hand opponent cue-bid three hearts, showing a sound raise in spades, and Chun attempted to cause confusion by bidding 3NT. The bidding continued in this way:

SOUTH	WEST	NORTH	EAST
Camacho	Chiu	Janz	Chun
1♠	3♢ (1)	3♡ (2)	3NT
4♣	Pass	Pass	5♢
5♠	Pass	Pass	?

(1) Hearts and diamonds.
(2) Sound raise to three spades (at least).

What should East do now? Normally you would be well content to have pushed the opponents to the five level. Partner is likely to be very short in spades, though, and you do have five-card support for one of his suits.

You might pass, you might bid six diamonds. Another possibility is six clubs, seeking to maintain the illusion that you have the best hand at the table.

(1) Pass   (2) 6♣   (3) 6♢

North–South game
Dealer South

	♠ K 6 3 2	
	♡ K 6	
	◇ Q 10 3	
	♣ A Q J 4	

♠ –		♠ J 10 5
♡ Q 8 7 5 3 2	N	♡ J
◇ A J 9 8 6	W E	◇ K 7 5 4 2
♣ 10 5	S	♣ 9 7 6 2

	♠ A Q 9 8 7 4	
	♡ A 10 9 4	
	◇ –	
	♣ K 8 3	

SOUTH	WEST	NORTH	EAST
Camacho	Chiu	Janz	Chun
1♠	3◇	3♡	3NT
4♠	Pass	Pass	5◇
5♠	Pass	Pass	6◇
6♠	Pass	Pass	7◇
Pass	Pass	7♠	All Pass

Not only did Chun bid six diamonds, he continued to seven diamonds over Camacho's six spades. Surely this was the end of the matter, you might think. No, Camacho made a forcing pass, to indicate his first-round diamond control. Janz, the Brazilian North, could now be fairly sure that his partner held the missing key cards. He bid the grand slam in spades and this contract proved to be cold. Chun had chased the Brazilians from a contract worth 710 into one worth 2210.

Suspense, suspense . . . how are we going to mark it? Does the six-diamond bid deserve any sympathy, do you think? Not really. When the opponents reach the five level you have two chances of gaining – they may be one too high, they may be one too low. It is very rarely right to bid again and we make it:

Pass–5,   6♣–1,   6◇–0

At the other table the Hong Kong North–South ground to a halt in five spades, the Brazilians gaining 17 IMPs.

48. Fourth to Speak!

Sweden met USA in one semi-final of the 1992 Olympiad. The match was some 9 boards old when Fallenius, North for Sweden, picked up this hand:

♠ A J
♡ A K 7
◇ J 3 2
♣ A J 7 6 3

Eighteen points, yes, but all three players had bid before it was his turn:

SOUTH	WEST	NORTH	EAST
Nilsland	Rodwell	Fallenius	Meckstroth
–	–	–	1NT (1)
3♠	4◇	?	

(1) 9–12 points.

His side was vulnerable, so Fallenius could expect his partner to hold good playing strength, if not a high point-count. What would you have bid with his hand?

It would surely be premature to double non-vulnerable opponents, since you have a comfortable game your way at least. Could there be a slam? If your thoughts are turning in that direction you could bid five spades, or a direct six spades. It is by no means certain that partner would treat four hearts as a cue-bid in support of spades, so best not to risk that. Our list has a slightly monotonous air:

(1) 4♠   (2) 5♠   (3) 6♠

North–South game
Dealer East

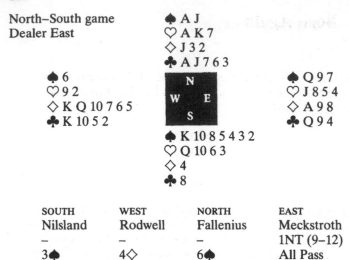

♠ A J
♡ A K 7
◇ J 3 2
♣ A J 7 6 3

♠ 6
♡ 9 2
◇ K Q 10 7 6 5
♣ K 10 5 2

♠ Q 9 7
♡ J 8 5 4
◇ A 9 8
♣ Q 9 4

♠ K 10 8 5 4 3 2
♡ Q 10 6 3
◇ 4
♣ 8

SOUTH	WEST	NORTH	EAST
Nilsland	Rodwell	Fallenius	Meckstroth
–	–	–	1NT (9–12)
3♠	4◇	6♠	All Pass

Nilsland was surprisingly weak for his vulnerable three-spade bid (we hardly dare imagine how little he would need to bid two spades). North was entitled to raise to six spades, and this bid has our full support:

$$4♠-1, \quad 5♠-3, \quad 6♠-5$$

Against six spades Rodwell attacked with a club, won in the dummy. Aiming to set up the clubs, declarer ruffed a club, then crossed to the ace of trumps and called for the trump jack. Meckstroth, who had opened 1NT, realised that declarer would guess the trumps right. If the jack were allowed to win declarer would remain in dummy, well placed to ruff another club. Meckstroth therefore covered the jack with the queen.

This thoughtful defence brought no dividend. Nilsland drew the last trump, crossed to ♡A to ruff a club, then ran the trumps. There was no squeeze, but the Swede guessed correctly to finesse ♡10 on the third round. Twelve tricks.

At the other table (and at both tables of the France–Netherlands semi-final) West opened three diamonds in the third seat. One North doubled, two Norths bid 3NT. It made little difference, the final contract in every case was just four spades.

49. Born Again

France and USA reached the final of the 1992 Olympiad. The French were leading by some 40 IMPs when Jeff Meckstroth picked up this hand:

        ♠ Q 6 4
        ♡ K 10 9 6 2
        ◇ –
        ♣ K 10 8 6 2

His partner, Eric Rodwell, opened one diamond. They were playing a 9–12 1NT when non-vulnerable, so the opening showed either a diamond suit or a 13–15 balanced hand. Meckstroth responded one heart and passed his partner's rebid of one spade (the opener's strength was limited since he had not opened a strong club). The auction was not yet over:

SOUTH	WEST	NORTH	EAST
Meckstroth	Perron	Rodwell	Chemla
–	–	1◇ (1)	Pass
1♡	Pass	1♠	Pass
Pass	2◇	Pass	3◇
?			

(1) Diamonds, or 13–15 balanced hand.

You might pass now, or perhaps compete with a double (not for penalties, since the opponents have found a fit at a low level). Two other possibilities are to offer delayed support for partner's spades, or perhaps to introduce your club suit. Which would be your choice?

(1) Pass   (2) Double   (3) 3♠   (4) 4♣

East–West game
Dealer North

                          ♠ A K 7 5
                          ♡ 8 4
                          ◇ 5 4 2
                          ♣ A Q 5 3

    ♠ 10 3   ♠ J 9 8 2
    ♡ J 3   N   ♡ A Q 7 5
    ◇ A Q J 10 9 7 3   W   E   ◇ K 8 6
    ♣ J 7   S   ♣ 9 4

                          ♠ Q 6 4
                          ♡ K 10 9 6 2
                          ◇ –
                          ♣ K 10 8 6 2

SOUTH	WEST	NORTH	EAST
Meckstroth	Perron	Rodwell	Chemla
–	–	1◇	Pass
1♡	Pass	1♠	Pass
Pass	2◇	Pass	3◇
4♣	4◇	5♣	All Pass

Rodwell's pass over two diamonds indicated fewer than three
hearts and the opponents' enthusiasm for diamonds suggested that
Rodwell would hold at most four diamonds, probably only three.
It was a bold effort but Meckstroth bid 4♣, netting a splendid
+420. A double might have located the club fit too. We mark it:

Pass–1,   Double–4,   3♠–2,   4♣–5

The USA fared poorly at the other table:

SOUTH	WEST	NORTH	EAST
Levy	Rosenberg	Mouiel	Deutsch
–	–	1♣	Pass
1♡	2◇	Pass	2♡
4♣	Pass	5♣	5◇
Pass	Pass	Dble	All Pass

East did too much and it seemed that the Americans might
suffer an unsightly −800. Mouiel started with the ace and king of
spades, though, and Rosenberg could now dispose of his heart
loser on dummy's spades. In the end only 2 IMPs to the French.

50. Trust to the Limit

The multi-coloured two diamond opening certainly adds to the excitement of the game, triggering many unforeseen situations. Few can be stranger than this one, which created a problem for the Brazilian player, Mello, playing against Norway in the 1993 Bermuda Bowl. This was his hand:

♠ 9 6 5 2
♡ A Q 5 3
♢ J 6 3
♣ J 7

With North–South vulnerable the auction started like this:

SOUTH	WEST	NORTH	EAST
–	–	–	2♢ (1)
Pass	5♢	Pass	Pass
6♣	Pass	?	

(1) Multi, weak two in either major or various strong hands.

Knowing that the 2♢ bid is forcing, your partner has passed on the first round, then, vulnerable against not, has come in with six clubs! What type of hand do you think he has? A one-suiter, or could he perhaps have a two-suiter? Presumably, at the score, he has serious hopes of making twelve tricks. Could your ace of hearts conceivably justify a raise to seven clubs?

These seem to be the possibilities:

(1) Pass   (2) 6♢   (3) 7♣

North–South game
Dealer East

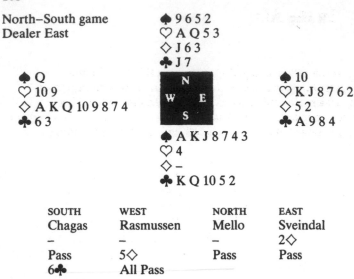

♠ 9 6 5 2
♡ A Q 5 3
♢ J 6 3
♣ J 7

♠ Q
♡ 10 9
♢ A K Q 10 9 8 7 4
♣ 6 3

♠ 10
♡ K J 8 7 6 2
♢ 5 2
♣ A 9 8 4

♠ A K J 8 7 4 3
♡ 4
♢ –
♣ K Q 10 5 2

SOUTH	WEST	NORTH	EAST
Chagas	Rasmussen	Mello	Sveindal
–	–	–	2♢
Pass	5♢	Pass	Pass
6♣	All Pass		

As you see, partner has made a rather eccentric pair of calls.
He was hoping you could deduce from his silence on the first
round that he held a marked two-suiter. Without support for clubs
you were expected to bid six diamonds, waiting to hear which
major partner held.

This was too deep for Mello but, as it happens, all turned out
well. West led ♢A against six clubs, reducing declarer to the
same trump length as East. However, when declarer played on
trumps Sveindal won immediately with the ace and, instead of
destroying the contract by continuing with diamonds, switched to
his singleton spade. No doubt he could scarcely believe that
Chagas held only five trumps. The Brazilian maestro gratefully
drew trumps and claimed the contract. East should surely have
ducked the first round of trumps. When he won the next round he
would know the situation.

How shall we mark this one? It does seem that a defender with
a one-suiter would have little reason to pass on the first round. On
that basis 6♢ by North is best. We make it:

Pass–2,   6♢–5,   7♣–1

51. In the Air

There was a rather unusual sequence on this deal from a Championship promoted by Icelandic Air. It was an important event, which attracted such stars as Zia Mahmood and his American partner, Larry Cohen.

On one board, with North–South vulnerable, the bidding started:

SOUTH	WEST	NORTH	EAST
–	–	1♣	1♡
2◇	4♡	6♣	Pass
Pass	Dble	Pass	Pass
?			

Zia, who was South, held:

♠ Q 9 3
♡ A J
◇ K Q 9 8 7 5 3
♣ Q

He has good support for a club contract: the queen of clubs and the ace of hearts seem to be excellent cards. What should he do now, do you think? If he is happy with the present contract he can pass; if he is *very* happy, he can even redouble. Should it seem advisable to move the contract elsewhere, he may bid either six diamonds or six no-trumps.

Which of these options appeals to you most:

(1) Pass   (2) Redouble   (3) 6◇   (4) 6NT

North–South game   ♠ A 2
Dealer North   ♡ –
                     ♢ J 6 4
                     ♣ A K 10 9 8 6 4 3

♠ K 8 7 4   ♠ J 10 6 5
♡ Q 9 8 5 4 2   N   ♡ K 10 7 6 3
♢ –   W   E   ♢ A 10 2
♣ J 5 2   S   ♣ 7

                  ♠ Q 9 3
                  ♡ A J
                  ♢ K Q 9 8 7 5 3
                  ♣ Q

SOUTH	WEST	NORTH	EAST
Zia		Cohen	
–	–	1♣	1♡
2♢	4♡	6♣	Pass
Pass	Dble	Pass	Pass
6♢	All Pass		

It was fairly certain that West's double was Lightner, asking for
a surprise lead; fairly certain, too, that the surprise would be a
void in diamonds. If this were so, then six diamonds might well be
a better spot. Since partner had opened just one club, then rebid
six clubs on the strength of your response in diamonds, he was
very likely to hold some length in diamonds. There is little merit
in the alternatives, so we mark as follows:

    Pass–1,   Redouble–0,   6♢–5,   6NT–1

Lightner doubles were devised in 1929, but whether, over the
years, they have shown a net profit is doubtful, Here, for
example, if West had not doubled, a clever East might have
thought along the lines we mentioned above: 'To jump to six
clubs North must have diamond support; I think I'll lead ♢A;
partner must be short and may hold a singleton or void.'
    The play in six diamonds is not so easy as it looks. Zia won the
heart lead, throwing a spade, then played ♢K, which held, ♣Q
and ♢Q. East won and forced dummy's last trump, but there was
no defence when winning clubs were played.

52. Did You Hear Me, Partner?

If you play chess at a modest level, what chance would you ever have of playing a grandmaster such as Kasparov or Karpov? Only in your dreams. It is one of the attractions of bridge that two novice players can enter a big tournament and perhaps find themselves at the same table as Omar Sharif or Zia Mahmood.

Even at international level the relative minnows meet the sharks. Hoping that we have not caused offence by this setting, the present deal features a clash between the mighty Italians, Belladonna and Garozzo, and a pair from CAC (a combined team from Central America and the Caribbean).

East, the dealer, opened one spade and South – with only the opponents vulnerable – held:

♠ 3
♡ K J 9 7 4 3
◇ K 10 9 8 5 2
♣ –

He had a gadget available – three clubs, to show a red two-suiter. The bidding continued:

SOUTH	WEST	NORTH	EAST
–	–	–	1♠
3♣ (1)	3♠	Pass	4♠
?			

(1) Hearts and diamonds.

The three-club overcall did not promise a 6–6 hand and you have to consider now whether you are worth another move. The options are Pass, 4NT to request partner to choose a suit, five clubs or five diamonds. What's your verdict?

(1) Pass   (2) 4NT   (3) 5♣   (4) 5◇

East–West game
Dealer East

```
                    ♠ J 5 4
                    ♡ 5
                    ♢ A 7
                    ♣ A 10 7 6 5 4 2
    ♠ K Q 7 6              N          ♠ A 10 9 8 2
    ♡ Q 6             W         E     ♡ A 10 8 2
    ♢ Q 6 4                            ♢ J 3
    ♣ J 9 8 3              S          ♣ K Q
                    ♠ 3
                    ♡ K J 9 7 4 3
                    ♢ K 10 9 8 5 2
                    ♣ –
```

SOUTH	WEST	NORTH	EAST
–	–	–	1♠
3♣	3♠	Pass	4♠
4NT	Pass	5♣	Dble
5♢	Dble	All Pass	

Five diamonds doubled was down two, 300 to East–West. This proved to be an expensive venture when at the other table North–South doubled four spades and collected 500 after a diamond lead.

At one time it was considered a capital offence to bid again after having pre-empted. South's two suits are poor and his partner is still there, perhaps intending to double four spades. This is how we mark the possible calls:

Pass–5,   4NT–1,   5♣–2,   5♢–0

The only reason we allow two points for 5♣ is that showing the club void may assist partner in the later bidding or play.

So, a poor effort by the CAC pair, then? No, in fact it was Garozzo who sat South with Belladonna North!

Most remarkable of all, only two of seven expert players in the South seat refrained from bidding again after they had shown their two-suiter. Was it really so tempting after overcalling at the three level on this rubbish?

53. Choice of Poisons

Poland led the USA when the last quarter of the 1994 Rosenblum Cup began. The Americans then did well at both tables and by the time board 62 went up on the screen – just three boards to play – they led by 24 IMPs. Almost all over, you might think, but then Rosenberg, South at Love All, picked up these cards:

```
♠ J 6 4
♡ K 5
♢ J 6
♣ K J 10 4 3 2
```

He was fourth to speak and bidding started:

SOUTH	WEST	NORTH	EAST
Rosenberg	Gawrys	Bates	Lasocki
–	Pass	Pass	1♡
2♣	4♡	Dble	Pass
Pass	Rdble	Pass	Pass
?			

Rosenberg's two clubs was a poorish overcall, most people would say, but when you know your opponents make that sort of bid you may feel you have to keep up with them. His partner's double was competitive, rather than a penalty double, suggesting values in the unbid suits – spades and diamonds.

Things have taken an ugly turn. You can be fairly sure that West, who redoubled, expects to make four hearts and will know how to deal with five clubs. There should be some sort of fit in spades, but J x x is a miserable combination opposite such as A x x x. There are only three possibilities, none of them attractive:

(1) Pass   (2) 4♠   (3) 5♣

Love all
Dealer West

♠ K 7 3 2
♡ 10 6
♢ K Q 9 8 2
♣ 9 6

♠ A 10 8
♡ 9 8 4 2
♢ 10 7 5 3
♣ A Q

```
    N
 W     E
    S
```

♠ Q 9 5
♡ A Q J 7 3
♢ A 4
♣ 8 7 5

♠ J 6 4
♡ K 5
♢ J 6
♣ K J 10 4 3 2

SOUTH	WEST	NORTH	EAST
Rosenberg	Gawrys	Bates	Lasocki
–	Pass	Pass	1♡
2♣	4♡	Dble	Pass
Pass	Rdble	Pass	Pass
4♠	Dble	All Pass	

As you see, the Americans had dug themselves into a pit. The 2♣ overall was borderline and North's competitive double, as we see it, extremely dubious on just a king and a king–queen. Although four hearts redoubled would no doubt have been made, a pass seems best to us on Rosenberg's hand. His ♡K is a good card and his other values may produce a second defensive trick. Had North had his double, four hearts might have failed.

Neither four spades nor five clubs will provide much change from 800 and we mark the alternatives:

Pass–5,   4♠–2,   5♣–1

Rosenberg went four down in four spades doubled – 800 away. As it happens, this was marginally better than paying out 880 to four hearts redoubled.

At the other table Stansby played sedately in four hearts and the Poles gained 9 IMPs, reducing the margin to 15. They had chances for a game swing on the next deal, but it went the other way and the final margin was 141–110 to the Americans.

54. A Possible Guide

Playing in the Rosenblum Cup, a teams event held at the World Pairs Olympiad, you pick up these South cards at Love All:

♠ J
♡ Q J 9 4 3 2
♢ A Q 7
♣ A J 6

East deals and passes, you open one heart, and the bidding continues:

SOUTH	WEST	NORTH	EAST
–	–	–	Pass
1♡	1♠	Dble	4♠
?			

Your partner's double was negative and, after the opponents' antics in spades, you can expect him to hold 9 or 10 cards in the minors. Which of the following alternatives impresses you most?

(1) Pass   (2) Double   (3) 4NT   (4) 5♣

Love all
Dealer East

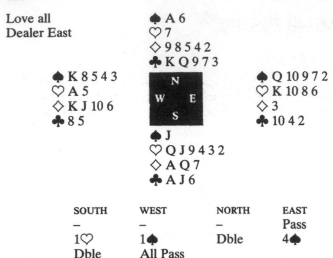

♠ A 6
♡ 7
♢ 9 8 5 4 2
♣ K Q 9 7 3

♠ K 8 5 4 3
♡ A 5
♢ K J 10 6
♣ 8 5

♠ Q 10 9 7 2
♡ K 10 8 6
♢ 3
♣ 10 4 2

♠ J
♡ Q J 9 4 3 2
♢ A Q 7
♣ A J 6

SOUTH	WEST	NORTH	EAST
–	–	–	Pass
1♡	1♠	Dble	4♠
Dble	All Pass		

This is a hand where the *Law of Total Tricks* may assist. East–West are likely to hold 10 cards in their trump suit (spades) and North–South 8 (either 6–2 in hearts or 5–3 in a minor). So, the two sides between them can score around 18 tricks (10 + 8). If North–South can make 11 their way, East–West will make only 7 in spades. And if North–South can make only 10, going one down in five of a minor, East–West will still go two down in 4♠. It follows that in both cases a double by South is a big winner.

Should you be suspicious of such calculations, 4NT (giving partner a choice of minors) is better than 5♣. We score it:

Pass–3,   Double–5,   4NT–1,   5♣–0

At the table four spades doubled was two down, North scoring a heart ruff. South went one down in four hearts at the other table, so the decision to double brought in 8 IMPs.

Look back to the hand diagram for a moment. You may think that five clubs was not too bad a contract and would have made, had East held such as ♢ K x. But then four spades doubled would have gone *three* down. You would make 11 tricks, they would make 7. As if by magic, the total would still come to 18.

55. Mixed Blessing

In the 1994 European Mixed Pairs Championships Alain Lévy of France partnered his glamorous compatriot, Danielle Gaviard. The chance of a medal was looming as Lévy, sitting North, picked up:

♠ A 9 7 2
♡ 4
♢ A K J 10 5
♣ A 6 3

With only his side vulnerable, the bidding began:

SOUTH	WEST	NORTH	EAST
–	1♡	Dble	Pass
4♠	Pass	?	

What now? You have something to spare for your double, obviously, and if you decide to advance there are various options available. You might employ Roman Key-Card Blackwood, make a cue-bid in the opponent's suit (five hearts), or perhaps raise to five of the trump suit. If you reckon science is inappropriate in a mixed pairs . . . you could simply jump to six spades.

A bid of five clubs would be fine, if a cue-bid showing spade support, but many would construe it as natural. Best to play safe there, perhaps, which leaves us with this list:

(1) Pass   (2) 4NT   (3) 5♡   (4) 5♠   (5) 6♠

North–South game
Dealer West

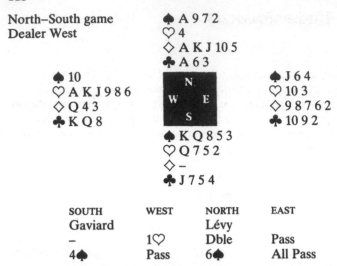

```
                      ♠ A 9 7 2
                      ♡ 4
                      ◇ A K J 10 5
                      ♣ A 6 3
♠ 10                                    ♠ J 6 4
♡ A K J 9 8 6                           ♡ 10 3
◇ Q 4 3                                 ◇ 9 8 7 6 2
♣ K Q 8                                 ♣ 10 9 2
                      ♠ K Q 8 5 3
                      ♡ Q 7 5 2
                      ◇ –
                      ♣ J 7 5 4
```

SOUTH	WEST	NORTH	EAST
Gaviard		Lévy	
–	1♡	Dble	Pass
4♠	Pass	6♠	All Pass

At the time there was some criticism of North's leap to six spades. We see little wrong with it – if anyone overbid, it was South. North might have used Roman Key-Card Blackwood to check that the partnership was not missing both ♡A and ♠K; no double he reckoned that the trump king, if missing, would succumb to a finesse. A bid of 5♣ would ask the wrong question: whether or not partner has a heart control. We mark it:

Pass–0,   4NT–5,   5♡–3,   5♠–0,   6♠–4

The play in six spades was interesting. West led ♡K and switched to ♣K, won by dummy's ace. Gaviard cashed ◇ A K, throwing clubs, then ruffed a diamond, felling the queen.

If East's length signals (♡10 and ♣2) were to be believed, she held 3–2–5–3 shape. Gaviard drew one round of trumps with the king, ruffed a heart low, then cashed the two established diamonds, throwing a heart and her last club. She now ruffed a club and ruffed her last heart with the ace, leaving her ♠ Q 8 triumphantly poised over East's ♠ J 6. Inspired by this brilliant effort, the French pair went on to win the bronze medal.

56.   Undue Modesty

The Daily Bulletins during a big event have to be written
overnight for the breakfast trade, and the standard of such
publications is variable. One deal from the world championship at
Albuquerque provided excellent copy, though. There were no
fewer than three stories concerning a deal where both sides were
vulnerable and South held:

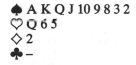

♠ A K Q J 10 9 8 3 2
♥ Q 6 5
♦ 2
♣ –

   The hand is from the Pairs and, as you may imagine, the field is
strong. East, on your right, deals and opens one diamond.

SOUTH	WEST	NORTH	EAST
–	–	–	1♦
?			

   It may seem obvious to overcall four spades now. Perhaps there
is tactical advantage to some lesser spade bid, though? A 1♠
overcall is hardly likely to be passed out, nor is a weak-jump
overcall of 2♠. Starting in this way may cause the opponents to
misjudge the situation later. Even a bizarre Pass, intending to
enter later, could work well against a certain class of opponent.
   Which of these actions strikes you as the most sensible?

(1) Pass   (2) Double   (3) 1♠   (4) 2♠   (5) 4♠

120

Game all   ♠ 7
Dealer East   ♡ 10 9 7 4
                  ◇ J 6 3
                  ♣ A 8 6 5 3

♠ 6 5   ♠ 4
♡ A 8 2   N   ♡ K J 3
◇ K 9   W   E   ◇ A Q 10 8 7 5 4
♣ K Q 10 9 7 4 S   ♣ J 2

                  ♠ A K Q J 10 9 8 3 2
                  ♡ Q 6 5
                  ◇ 2
                  ♣ –

SOUTH	WEST	NORTH	EAST
–	–	–	1◇
Pass (!)	2♣	Pass	2◇
2♠	Pass	Pass	3◇
4♠	5◇	Pass	Pass
5♠	Dble	All Pass	

Roudinesco passed initially, then bid all the way to five spades. West led ♣K and declarer's diamond loser went away. When ♡10 was led from dummy East made the mistake of playing low (he must rise with the king to beat the contract). The 10 forced West's ace and dummy's ♠7 provided an entry for a heart lead towards the queen. +850 gave North–South an 84% score.

Does this result vindicate Roudinesco's tactics? We don't think so. Starting with a Pass or low call, then bidding to the skies, may fool players at the club down the road; an experienced opponent will realise immediately that you have a good hand. An immediate four spades puts West under more pressure – he might well double. We award these marks:

   Pass–1,   Double–1,   1♠–2,   2♠–1,   4♠–5

Pacault, of France, passed over 1◇, over 2◇, and then over 3◇! He collected –150 for his pains, a poor score. Meanwhile, Jaggy Shivdasani sat South and led ♠2 against East's six diamonds! His partner won coolly with the 7 and played ace and another club. Two down, but still not so good as buying the contract in 4♠.

57. Raising the Bar

In the 1994 Grand National Final, in the US, a New York team
(Berkowitz, Cayne, Cohen and Sontag) faced the Midwest
(Johnson, Simson, Meckstroth and Rodwell). On one deal in the
second quarter the East players held:

♠ K 5 4
♡ 10
◇ 10 8 7 6
♣ K 9 6 5 3

The score was Game All and the auction at both tables started
like this:

SOUTH	WEST	NORTH	EAST
–	–	1♡	Pass
1♠	2♣	Dble (1)	?

(1) Support double, any strength with 3-card spade support.

Using opener's double of an overcall to show 3-card support for
partner is a method that has gained considerable popularity
recently. The main advantage, of course, is that a direct raise
promises at least four trumps; partner can then judge more
accurately how high he should compete.

Now look at the East hand. Remembering that the score is
Game All, you must decide how high to raise the bar in clubs. Or
is there any merit in a Pass, keeping the club fit under wraps? This
is the list:

(1) Pass   (2) 3♣   (3) 4♣   (4) 5♣

Game all   ♠ A 9 8
Dealer North   ♡ A J 8 7 3
               ◇ K Q J 4 2
               ♣ –

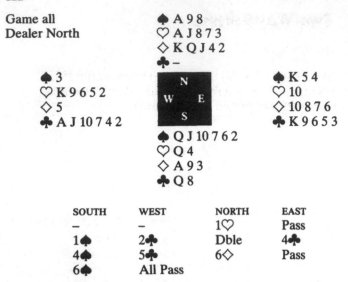

♠ 3   ♠ K 5 4
♡ K 9 6 5 2   ♡ 10
◇ 5   ◇ 10 8 7 6
♣ A J 10 7 4 2   ♣ K 9 6 5 3

               ♠ Q J 10 7 6 2
               ♡ Q 4
               ◇ A 9 3
               ♣ Q 8

SOUTH	WEST	NORTH	EAST
–	–	1♡	Pass
1♠	2♣	Dble	4♣
4♠	5♣	6◇	Pass
6♠	All Pass		

At one table East bid only 4♣ and North–South reached six
spades. Declarer ruffed the club lead and played ♠9 to the
queen, East ducking. Best now is to ruff the last club and return
to ◇A to play a second trump. This line fails only if East holds
three trumps to the king and only two diamonds: he would be
able to lock declarer in dummy with his second diamond.

Missing this line, South relied on the heart finesse. When West
failed to cover ♡Q declarer ruffed a club, returned to ◇A, and
played a second trump. Any return from East would now give
declarer an easy entry to his hand to draw the last trump; 1430 to
North–South.

At the other table East raised boldly to *five* clubs. South could
do no more than double and the pickings were modest – just 200.
It was the right time to pre-empt and we give these marks:

      Pass–1,   3♣–1,   4♣–3,   5♣–5

Over 4♣ you fully expect one or other opponent to bid 4♠ (at
least). You will then be faced with a further decision, whether to
sacrifice. By bidding 5♣ immediately you transfer the last
decision to your opponents. Let them guess wrongly!

58. Two-Way Finesse

There was exciting action on the very first board of the 1995 Macallan/Sunday Times International Pairs. Paul Chemla sat North at Love All and picked up these cards:

♠ K J 5 3
♡ Q 10 6 5 3
♢ K 4
♣ Q 8

This was the start to the auction:

SOUTH	WEST	NORTH	EAST
Mari	Chagas	Chemla	Lombardi
–	Pass	Pass	1♡
1♠	2♠ (1)	?	

(1) Sound raise to three hearts at least.

You have good support for partner's spades and could express this with one of three bids – three hearts, three spades or four spades. The opponents are bidding strongly in hearts, though. If you think it would be more productive to double them in some number of hearts, you may prefer to pass at this stage.

A double of two spades would suggest a doubleton spade honour and request a spade lead rather than invite partner to compete in the suit. Not much point in that, so we will restrict the list to:

(1) Pass   (2) 3♡   (3) 3♠   (4) 4♠

124

Love all
Dealer West

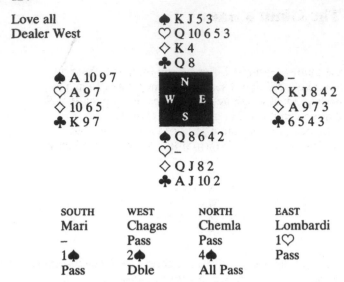

♠ K J 5 3
♡ Q 10 6 5 3
◇ K 4
♣ Q 8

♠ A 10 9 7
♡ A 9 7
◇ 10 6 5
♣ K 9 7

♠ –
♡ K J 8 4 2
◇ A 9 7 3
♣ 6 5 4 3

♠ Q 8 6 4 2
♡ –
◇ Q J 8 2
♣ A J 10 2

SOUTH	WEST	NORTH	EAST
Mari	Chagas	Chemla	Lombardi
–	Pass	Pass	1♡
1♠	2♠	4♠	Pass
Pass	Dble	All Pass	

Chemla could tell that his partner would be void in hearts. With every chance of only three losers elsewhere, he leapt to 4♠. You won't find us disagreeing with this valuation and we mark it:

Pass–1,   3♡–2,   3♠–1,   4♠–5

Chagas doubled four spades and led ♡A, ruffed by declarer. After a diamond to the king and ace East returned a diamond, South winning the queen. A trump to the king revealed the bad break and Mari now led dummy's ♣Q. When East failed to cover, declarer concluded that West must hold the club king. He overtook the queen with the ace, discarded a club on ◇J, and took a ruffing finesse with the J 10. This manoeuvre succeeded handsomely and Mari made ten tricks on a crossruff.

As happens in these times, there were those who rated both the West and the North hands worth an opening bid. Robson opened 1♠ as West and Forrester's 1NT response ended the auction, Four heart tricks and a trick in each of the other suits netted the British pair a top East–West score of +90.

59. The Giant's Axe

One of the many pleasures this game can bring is to hear an opponent make a bid that it seems you can penalise heavily. Sometimes you must weigh up whether the likely penalty will match what you could collect under your own steam.

That's the decision that Ian McCance faced in the 1995 Australian National Open Teams. Sitting West, he held these cards:

♠ A Q J 8
♡ K 7
♢ A J 5 3 2
♣ A 8

His partner opened a weak two in hearts and the next player, vulnerable against not, stepped in with two spades:

SOUTH	WEST	NORTH	EAST
–	–	–	2♡ (1)
2♠	?		

(1) Weak, 6–10 points

South has entered the auction on a suit at best headed by the K 10 9. With four likely trump tricks, two aces, and partner's weak two to come, a fair penalty seems likely. An alternative is to bid game in hearts. Or, if you think that twelve tricks are at all likely, you could make a relay response of 2NT; your partner will then tell you whether he is maximum or minimum and whether he holds two of the top three trump honours. These are the possibilities:

(1) Double   (2) 2NT (relay)   (3) 4♡

North–South game
Dealer East

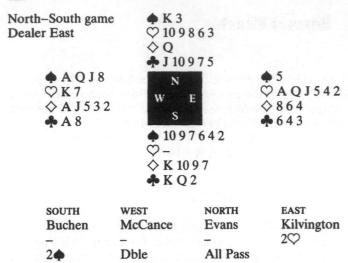

```
                       ♠ K 3
                       ♡ 10 9 8 6 3
                       ◇ Q
                       ♣ J 10 9 7 5
  ♠ A Q J 8                              ♠ 5
  ♡ K 7              N                   ♡ A Q J 5 4 2
  ◇ A J 5 3 2    W       E               ◇ 8 6 4
  ♣ A 8              S                   ♣ 6 4 3
                       ♠ 10 9 7 6 4 2
                       ♡ –
                       ◇ K 10 9 7
                       ♣ K Q 2
```

SOUTH	WEST	NORTH	EAST
Buchen	McCance	Evans	Kilvington
–	–	–	2♡
2♠	Dble	All Pass	

Expecting to pick up least 500, McCance doubled and led ♡K. Dummy, with ♠K sitting over him, was not a pleasant sight. Declarer ruffed the heart lead and played a trump towards the king. West could score no more than three trumps and two aces and the contract romped home.

At the other table West judged the auction more successfully. His partner opened *three* hearts, South stepping in with three spades ('I was pre-balancing, partner'). This time West went for the plus score he could more or less guarantee, bidding four hearts. A bonus arrived when North felt he had enough to double this contract; West redoubled and his side duly collected 880 in addition to the 670 from the first table.

Many players would double 2♠ on McCance's cards and it was certainly unlucky that the contract should actually make. Nevertheless, it is unlikely that you will collect more than 500 against sound opponents and game in hearts is a near certainty.

Little harm could come from a 2NT enquiry, but even if partner admits to ♡ A Q and a maximum a slam would be a dubious venture. South's intervention, when holding so few high cards, suggests that the breaks will be bad. We make it:

Double–2,   2NT–3,   4♡–5

60. Beyond Reach

Many critical bidding decisions occur when both sides have an excellent fit. The following deal, a spectacular example, arose in a team tournament in Eindhoven. When the two leading teams met in the last round, the North players picked up:

♠ A K J 10 6 4
♡ K 10 5 4
♢ –
♣ 7 5 4

At one table South opened three hearts at favourable vulnerability and the next player passed. It was not likely that partner would hold the ace of hearts and a second round club control, so North contented himself with four hearts. The bidding was not yet over:

SOUTH	WEST	NORTH	EAST
3♡	Pass	4♡	5♢
Pass	Pass	5♡	Dble
Pass	6♢	?	

Time to think again. The chances are fair that two spade tricks will stand up against a diamond contract. It might perhaps have been a good idea to respond three spades on the first round. That would suggest a good opening lead, perhaps also help partner to judge the subsequent auction.

Too late for that now. Should you double, telling partner not to bid on, or take one more push to six hearts? If you're not sure what to do you can pass, leaving the decision to partner. These are the options:

(1) Pass   (2) Double   (3) 6♡

East–West game
Dealer South

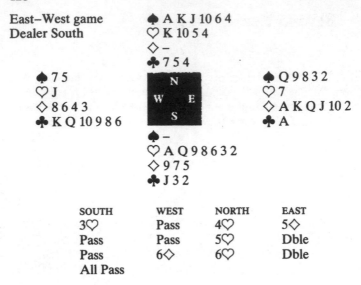

	♠ A K J 10 6 4		
	♡ K 10 5 4		
	◇ –		
	♣ 7 5 4		
♠ 7 5			♠ Q 9 8 3 2
♡ J			♡ 7
◇ 8 6 4 3			◇ A K Q J 10 2
♣ K Q 10 9 8 6			♣ A
	♠ –		
	♡ A Q 9 8 6 3 2		
	◇ 9 7 5		
	♣ J 3 2		

SOUTH	WEST	NORTH	EAST
3♡	Pass	4♡	5◇
Pass	Pass	5♡	Dble
Pass	6◇	6♡	Dble
All Pass			

Even if there are two or more top losers in clubs, six hearts might still make if a club is not led. Also, there is no guarantee that six diamonds will fail (as you see, South would have to underlead his ♡A). These are two powerful reasons for bidding six hearts and we mark it:

Pass–1,   Double–0,   6♡–5

West did lead a diamond and declarer ended with a doubled overtrick. As it happens, the blockage in clubs meant that six hearts would succeed even on a club lead. At the other table East was allowed to play in six diamonds. You would expect South to find the heart underlead, but . . . no, he decided to 'look at dummy', leading ♡A. He was soon looking at 1370 in the minus column, conceding a near maximum swing of 23 IMPs. A low heart lead puts the slam *three* down. North would cash ♠ A K and, slightly annoying for declarer, give partner a ruff with ◇9.

We mentioned that North might have responded 3♠ rather than 4♡. Another lively possibility was a direct 6♡, exerting maximum pressure on the opponents. Not so good if your partner is the sort who opens three hearts on ♡ J x x x x x, of course!